W9-ASX-307

STUDY GUIDE

Long Walk to Freedom
Nelson Mandela

WITH CONNECTIONS

HOLT, RINEHART AND WINSTON
Harcourt Brace & Company

Austin • New York • Orlando • Atlanta • San Francisco • Boston • Dallas • Toronto • London

Staff Credits

Director: Mescal Evler

Manager of Editorial Operations: Bill Wahlgren

Executive Editor: Katie Vignery

Book Editor: Carolyn Logan

Editorial Staff: *Managing Editor,* Marie Price; *Editorial Operations Coordinator,* Lori De La Garza; *Copyediting Manager,* Michael Neibergall; *Senior Copyeditor,* Mary Malone; *Copyeditors,* Joel Bourgeois, Liz Dickson, Gabrielle Field, Jane Kominek, Millicent Ondras, Theresa Reding, Désirée Reid, Kathleen Scheiner, Laurie Schlesinger; *Editorial Coordinators,* Diane Hardin, Heather Cheyne, Mark Holland, Marcus Johnson, Jill O'Neal, Kelly Tankersley, Janet Riley; *Word Processors,* Ruth Hooker, Margaret Sanchez, Gail Coupland

Permissions: Lee Noble, Catherine Paré

Design: *Design Director,* Joe Melomo; *Art Buyer Supervisor,* Elaine Tate

Prepress Production: Beth Prevelige, Simira Davis, Joan Lindsay

Manufacturing Coordinator: Michael Roche

Electronic Publishing: *Operators,* JoAnn Brown, Lana Knapp, Indira Konanur, Christopher Lucas, Nanda Patel; *Administrative Coordinator,* Sally Williams

For permission to reprint copyrighted material, grateful acknowledgment is made to the following source:

Little Brown and Company: From *Long Walk to Freedom: The Autobiography of Nelson Mandela.* Copyright © 1994 by Nelson Rolihlahla Mandela.

Cover: Cover illustration by Erin Cone/HRW. [photo reference: Paul Weinberg/Impact Visuals]

HRW is a trademark licensed to Holt, Rinehart and Winston, registered in the United States of America and/or other jurisdictions.

Printed in the United States of America

ISBN 0-03-056582-0

5 6 7 018 09 08 07 06

TABLE *of* CONTENTS

Using This Study Guide

Approaching the Book

The successful study of a book often depends on students' enthusiasm, curiosity, and openness. The ideas in **Introducing the Book** will help you create such a climate for your class. Background information in **About the Writer** and **About the Book** can also be used to pique students' interest.

Reading and Responding to the Book

Making Meanings questions are designed for both individual response and group or class discussion. They range from personal response to high-level critical thinking.

Reading Strategies worksheets contain graphic organizers. They help students explore techniques that enhance both comprehension and literary analysis. Many worksheets are appropriate for more than one set of chapters.

Book Notes provide high-interest information relating to historical, cultural, literary, and other elements of the book. The **Investigate** questions and **Reader's Log** ideas guide students to further research and consideration.

Choices suggest a wide variety of activities for exploring different aspects of the book, either individually or collaboratively. The results may be included in a portfolio or used as springboards for larger projects.

Glossary and Vocabulary (1) clarifies allusions and other references and (2) provides definitions students may refer to as they read. The **Vocabulary Worksheets** activities are based on the Vocabulary Words.

Reader's Log, Double-Entry Journal, and **Group Discussion Log** model formats and spark ideas for responding to the book. These pages are designed to be a resource for independent reading as well.

Responding to the Book as a Whole

The following features provide options for culminating activities that can be used in whole-class, small-group, or independent-study situations.

Book Review provides a format for summarizing and integrating the major literary elements.

Book Projects suggest multiple options for culminating activities. **Writing About the Book, Cross-Curricular Connections,** and **Multimedia and Internet Connections** propose project options that extend the text into other genres, content areas, and environments.

Responding to the Connections

Making Meanings questions in **Exploring the Connections** facilitate discussion of the additional readings in the HRW LIBRARY edition of this book.

This Study Guide is intended to

- *provide maximum versatility and flexibility*
- *serve as a ready resource for background information on both the author and the book*
- *act as a catalyst for discussion, analysis, interpretation, activities, and further research*
- *provide reproducible masters that can be used for either individual or collaborative work, including discussions and projects*
- *provide multiple options for evaluating students' progress through the book and the Connections*

Literary Elements

- plot structure
- major themes
- characterization
- setting
- point of view
- symbolism, irony, and other elements appropriate to the title

Making Meanings Reproducible Masters

- First Thoughts
- Shaping Interpretations
- Connecting with the Text
- Extending the Text
- Challenging the Text

A **Reading Check** focuses on review and comprehension.

The Worksheets Reproducible Masters

- Reading Strategies Worksheets
- Literary Elements Worksheets
- Vocabulary Worksheets

Reaching All Students

Because the questions and activities in this Study Guide are in the form of reproducible masters, labels indicating the targeted types of learners have been omitted.

Most classrooms include students from a variety of backgrounds and with a range of learning styles. The questions and activities in this Study Guide have been developed to meet diverse student interests, abilities, and learning styles. Of course, students are full of surprises, and a question or activity that is challenging to an advanced student can also be handled successfully by students who are less proficient readers. The interest level, flexibility, and variety of these questions and activities make them appropriate for a range of students.

Struggling Readers and Students with Limited English Proficiency:
The **Making Meanings** questions, the **Choices** activities, and the **Reading Strategies** worksheets all provide opportunities for students to check their understanding of the text and to review their reading. The **Book Projects** ideas are designed for a range of student abilities and learning styles. Both questions and activities motivate and encourage students to make connections to their own interests and experiences. The **Vocabulary Worksheets** can be used to facilitate language acquisition. **Dialogue Journals,** with you the teacher or with more advanced students as respondents, can be especially helpful to these students.

Advanced Students: The writing opportunity suggested with the **Making Meanings** questions and the additional research suggestions in **Book Notes** should offer a challenge to these students. The **Choices** and **Book Projects** activities can be taken to advanced levels. **Dialogue Journals** allow advanced students to act as mentors or to engage each other intellectually.

Auditory Learners: A range of suggestions in this Study Guide targets students who respond particularly well to auditory stimuli: making and listening to audiotapes and engaging in class discussion, role-playing, debate, oral reading, and oral presentation. See **Making Meanings** questions, **Choices,** and **Book Projects** options (especially **Cross-Curricular Connections** and **Multimedia and Internet Connections**).

Visual/Spatial Learners: Students are guided to create visual representations of text scenes and concepts and to analyze films or videos in **Choices** and in **Book Projects.** The **Reading Strategies** and **Literary Elements Worksheets** utilize graphic organizers as a way to both assimilate and express information.

Tactile/Kinesthetic Learners: The numerous interactive, hands-on, and problem-solving projects are designed to encourage the involvement of students motivated by action and movement. The projects also provide an opportunity for **interpersonal learners** to connect with others through book-related tasks. The **Group Discussion Log** will help students track the significant points of their interactions.

Verbal Learners: For students who naturally connect to the written and spoken word, the **Reader's Logs** and **Dialogue Journals** will have particular appeal. This Study Guide offers numerous writing opportunities: See **Making Meanings, Choices, Book Notes,** and **Writing About the Book** in **Book Projects.** These options should also be attractive to **intrapersonal learners.**

Assessment Options

Perhaps the most important goal of assessment is to provide feedback on the effectiveness of instructional strategies. As you monitor the degree to which your students understand and engage with the book, you will naturally adjust the frequency and ratio of class to small-group and verbal to nonverbal activities, as well as the extent to which direct teaching of reading strategies, literary elements, or vocabulary is appropriate to your students' needs.

If you are in an environment where **portfolios** contain only carefully chosen samples of students' writing, you may want to introduce a second, "working," portfolio and negotiate grades with students after examining all or selected items from this portfolio.

The features in this Study Guide are designed to facilitate a variety of assessment techniques.

Reader's Logs and Double-Entry Journals can be briefly reviewed and responded to (students may wish to indicate entries they would prefer to keep private). The logs and journals are an excellent measure of students' engagement with and understanding of the book.

Group Discussion Log entries provide students with an opportunity for self-evaluation of their participation in both book discussions and project planning.

Making Meanings questions allow you to observe and evaluate a range of student responses. Those who have difficulty with literal and interpretive questions may respond more completely to **Connecting** and **Extending**. The **Writing Opportunity** provides you with the option of ongoing assessment: You can provide feedback to students' brief written responses to these prompts as they progress through the book.

Reading Strategies Worksheets, Book Review, and Literary Elements Worksheets lend themselves well to both quick assessment and students' self-evaluation. They can be completed collaboratively and the results shared with the class, or students can compare their individual responses in a small-group environment.

Choices activities and writing prompts offer all students the chance to successfully complete an activity, either individually or collaboratively, and share the results with the class. These items are ideal for peer evaluation and can help prepare students for presenting and evaluating larger projects at the completion of the book unit.

Vocabulary Worksheets can be used as diagnostic tools or as part of a concluding test.

Book Projects evaluations might be based on the degree of understanding of the book demonstrated by the project. Students' presentations of their projects should be taken into account, and both self-evaluation and peer evaluation can enter into the overall assessment.

The **Test** is a traditional assessment tool in three parts: objective items, short-answer questions, and essay questions.

Questions for Self-evaluation and Goal Setting

- What are the three most important things I learned in my work with this book?
- How will I follow up so that I remember them?
- What was the most difficult part of working with this book?
- How did I deal with the difficulty, and what would I do differently?
- What two goals will I work toward in my reading, writing, group, and other work?
- What steps will I take to achieve those goals?

Items for a "Working" Portfolio

- reading records
- drafts of written work and project plans
- audio- and videotapes of presentations
- notes on discussions
- reminders of cooperative projects, such as planning and discussion notes
- artwork
- objects and mementos connected with themes and topics in the book
- other evidence of engagement with the book

For help with establishing and maintaining portfolio assessment, examine the **Portfolio Management System** *in* ELEMENTS OF LITERATURE.

Answer Key

The Answer Key at the back of this guide is not intended to be definitive or to set up a right-wrong dichotomy. In questions that involve interpretation, however, students' responses should be defended by citations from the text.

About the Writer

More on Mandela

Benson, Mary. **Nelson Mandela: The Man and the Movement.** New York: Norton, 1986.

Derrida, Jacques, and Mustapha Tlili, eds. **For Nelson Mandela.** New York: Seaver Books, 1987.

Frost, Brian. **Struggling to Forgive: Nelson Mandela and South Africa's Search for Reconciliation.** London: HarperCollins, 1998.

Gregory, James with Bob Graham. **Goodbye Bafana: Nelson Mandela, My Prisoner, My Friend.** London: Headline, 1995.

Martin, Meredith. **Nelson Mandela: A Biography.** New York: St. Martin's Press, 1998.

Ottaway, David. **Chained Together: Mandela, De Klerk, and the Struggle to Remake South Africa.** New York: Times Books, 1993.

Sampson, Anthony. **Mandela: The Authorized Biography.** New York: Knopf/Random House, 1999.

Waldmeir, Patti. **Anatomy of a Miracle: The End of Apartheid and the Birth of the New South Africa.** New York: Norton, 1997.

Also by Mandela

No Easy Walk to Freedom. Articles, speeches, and trial addresses. London: Heinemann, 1973.

The Struggle Is My Life. Speeches and writings, along with relevant historical documents and accounts given by fellow prisoners of Mandela in prison. New York: Pathfinder Press, 1986.

Nelson Mandela Speaks: Forging a Democratic Nonracial South Africa. Mandela's account of the end of apartheid. New York: Pathfinder, 1993.

A biography of Mandela appears in Long Walk to Freedom, *HRW LIBRARY edition. You may wish to share this additional information with your students.*

When Nelson Mandela was born in July 1918, his father gave him the African name "Rolihlahla," which, prophetically, means "troublemaker." Mandela's father, a chief in the Thembu tribe to which the family belonged, was himself considered a "troublemaker" by local white officials. Shortly after Nelson's birth his father was summoned by the magistrate, but sent the response "I will not come, I am still girding for battle." For this insubordination Mandela's father was deposed of his chieftainship. In his autobiography, Mandela reflects that "my father possessed a proud rebelliousness, a stubborn sense of fairness, that I recognize in myself."

These qualities, which would eventually carry Mandela to the South African presidency, were evident in the young Mandela as well. As a student at the University College of Fort Hare, Mandela became involved in a boycott protesting what the students considered an unsatisfactory diet by refusing to vote in the election for the Student Representative Council. Mandela was elected a student government representative twice by the few students who voted, but he refused to serve because he believed that he did not truly represent the whole student body. As a result, Mandela was suspended from the school.

Mandela's early professional life centered around his commitment to the underdog—who, in segregated, mid-twentieth-century South Africa, was the African. After receiving his law degree, Mandela, together with his good friend Oliver Tambo, opened the first black law partnership in Johannesburg. The two worked tirelessly to defend Africans who had committed "crimes" such as walking through a "Whites Only" entrance, being found on the streets past curfew, being unemployed, or being employed in the wrong place. As Mandela himself put it, "Working as a lawyer in South Africa meant operating under a debased system of justice, a code of law that did not enshrine equality but its opposite."

As an activist, a member of the African National Congress (ANC), and later as a political prisoner, Mandela refused to be debilitated by a system that he found skewed and prejudiced. When, for example, the ANC's philosophy of nonviolence seemed to be failing, Mandela persuaded the ANC to sponsor the formation of a military group—Umkhonto we Sizwe, or The Spear of the Nation—to plan and execute acts of violence against the state. Later, convicted of sabotage and treason and sentenced to life in prison, Mandela refused to submit. From the beginning of his nearly three decades behind bars, he insisted on being treated fairly: He refused to wear the short trousers given to Africans to remind them that they were "boys"; he campaigned first for study rights and then for desks and chairs in the prisoners' cells; and he quietly warned warders and prison officials when they broke regulations, often putting a stop to their abusive behavior.

Mandela was painfully aware of the conflict between his public and private lives, and he lamented that the choices he made were often at the expense of those he loved. His first marriage, to Evelyn Mase, suffered from Mandela's relentless work schedule during the early years of his involvement with the ANC, and finally ended in 1955 when Evelyn gave him an ultimatum—either the ANC or the marriage.

His second marriage, to Winifred Madikizela, lasted for almost thirty-four years. During his imprisonment, Winnie unswervingly advocated Nelson's release and developed quite a reputation of her own as a radical, even militant, freedom fighter. When the couple separated in 1992—according to Mandela, because of "tensions . . . owing to differences between our-selves"—Winnie had recently been embroiled in a kidnapping scandal and subsequently was banished from the freedom movement by members of the ANC. Still, Mandela contended that she was innocent and took responsibility for the failure of their mar-

riage. "When your life is the struggle," he writes, "there is little room left for family. That has always been my greatest regret, and the most painful aspect of the choice I made."

Often during his negotiations with the South African government, both before and after his release from prison, Mandela was forced to make other uncomfortable choices. His decision to instigate talks was made in isolation from other ANC members, partly due to the impossibility of securing their approval—he was being kept in separate quarters—and partly because, as he put it, if "matters went awry" the ANC would have a handy excuse: He had acted as an individual, not as a representative of the organization. Although his colleagues approved of his strategy when they learned about it, some would later criticize him for his "authoritarian tendencies," while other younger, more militant revolutionaries would mistrust his diplomacy and moderation as weaknesses.

Still, the legacy Mandela has left as the first black, democratically elected president of South Africa and the man largely responsible for the dismantling of apartheid is one of courage and selflessness in the face of adversity. As a testimony to this legacy, Mandela was awarded the Nobel Peace Prize in 1993, together with F. W. de Klerk, and he holds more than fifty honorary degrees from universities across the world. Today Mandela resides in Qunu, his childhood home.

Special Considerations

Possible sensitive issues in this book are racism, circumcision, the psychological and physical abuse of prisoners, and political violence.

For Viewing

Mandela and de Klerk. Hallmark Home Entertainment, 1997, rated PG-13. A docudrama originally produced for cable television, starring Sidney Poitier, Michael Caine, and Tina Lifford.

Mandela, Son of Africa, Father of a Nation. Palm Pictures, 1996, not rated. A documentary originally produced as a motion picture, providing a candid portrait of the man who became a legend. Oscar nominee, 1997, for best documentary.

Mandela's Fight for Freedom. Discovery Communication, 1995, not rated. The Discovery Channel's made-for-television documentary exploring Mandela's years in prison and the eventful years after his release.

The Speeches of Nelson Mandela. Mpi Home Video, 1995, not rated. Video containing seventy minutes of excerpts from Mandela's most important speeches.

Cry, the Beloved Country. Monterey Home Video, 1951, not rated. The story of a back-country minister who searches for his son in Johannesburg. Based on Alan Paton's book by the same name. A good introduction to apartheid.

For Listening

Long Walk to Freedom. Time Warner AudioBooks, 1994. An abridged recording of Mandela's autobiography.

Historical Context

The country of South Africa is located on the southernmost tip of the African continent. Although it is the richest, most economically and industrially developed nation in Africa, its wealth is very unevenly distributed. Whites, who are the country's minority, hold most of the wealth, while the majority of the population—blacks, people of Asian descent, and people of mixed race—own little.

The nation's economic imbalance is a product of its turbulent racial history. South Africa's European roots reach back to the mid-1600s, when it was colonized by powerful Dutch traders. The colony, known as the Cape Colony, was occupied by Dutch, French, and German people—many of them farmers, or *Boers,* who used native South Africans as slaves—until it came under British rule in 1814. When the British outlawed slavery in 1833, tensions increased between the Boers and their British rulers. These tensions grew over time and culminated in the Boer War, fought between 1899 and 1902. When the Boers finally surrendered, their territories became British colonies.

In spite of resistance from some black South African groups such as the Zulus, the white population ultimately extended its control over the entire region. In 1910 the Union of South Africa, a self-governing nation within the British Empire, was formed. Its constitution gave white citizens virtually complete power. In 1912, inspired by the Indian pacifist Mohandas Gandhi, a group of black South Africans founded the South African Native National Congress—later dubbed the African National Congress, or ANC—to fight for equal rights.

South Africa's first two prime ministers, Louis Botha and Jan Christiaan Smuts, attempted to unite the country's major white populations: the Afrikaners, descendants of the Boers, who spoke a Dutch-like language called Afrikaans, and the English-speaking whites. Many Afrikaners resisted, believing that they had a God-given right to rule South Africa, and in 1914 the National Party was formed to help realize this belief. Under the leadership of Barry Munnik Hertzog, the party won control of the government in 1924, and by 1931 many Afrikaner goals had been reached. In that year, South Africa gained full independence from Britain while remaining a member of the British Commonwealth of Nations. Hertzog's government seriously curtailed what little freedom blacks still had. Their voting rights were reduced, and laws were passed that dictated where they could live and what kinds of jobs they could have.

During World War II, the National Party floundered and Smuts was again elected the nation's prime minister. Under Smuts, South Africa joined forces with Britain, the United States, and the other Allied forces, but the National Party created internal unrest by opposing the alliance and sympathizing with Nazi Germany. The National Party returned to power in 1948 under the leadership of Daniel Malan, whose platform rested on the idea of the *swart gevaar,* or the "black danger." Preaching that if the whites did not keep the blacks under control the nation would break into a bloody civil war, Malan's government immediately began implementing *apartheid,* which literally means "apartness" in Afrikaans.

During the 1950s the ANC, which had joined forces with other oppressed nonwhite groups, led a campaign against the government's racial policies. Each effort was put down, often through police force, and by the early 1960s both the ANC and the Pan Africanist Congress (PAC), a strictly black-rights group, had been banned. Throughout the turbulent '60s and '70s opposition to apartheid grew, both within South Africa and throughout the international community. Under Prime Minister Pieter Botha in the late 1970s, the government began to repeal some of its apartheid laws. However, in 1984 the country adopted a new constitution allowing for equal representation of whites, mixed-race people, and Asians, while black South Africans remained unrepresented.

Many of the ensuing demonstrations and riots ended in bloody conflicts between blacks and state police, and the death toll mounted. Between 1985 and 1990 the country was declared to be in a state of emergency, which allowed the police to make random, often unprovoked arrests. But when F. W. de Klerk became state president in 1989, he realized that the nation was on the brink of a civil war and that minority rule could not continue. Over the next several years, in negotiations with Nelson Mandela (whom he released from prison in 1990) and against a backdrop of almost constant domestic violence, de Klerk took steps to dismantle apartheid. He also lifted the long-standing bans on the ANC and the PAC. Finally, after years of struggle, blacks were granted full voting rights by a new constitution adopted by the country in 1993. When the nation's first fully democratic elections were held in 1994, the ANC won almost two-thirds of the seats in the newly formed assembly, and Nelson Mandela was elected state president.

Origin of the Book

Much of *Long Walk to Freedom* was drafted during Mandela's lengthy prison sentence. On his fifty-seventh birthday, two of Mandela's comrades approached him and suggested that he write his memoirs. They argued that if the manuscript could be smuggled out and published—with luck, on Mandela's sixtieth birthday—it would inspire and encourage young people involved in the struggle against apartheid. Mandela agreed, and within four months the manuscript was completed. It was then transcribed into "microscopic shorthand" and safely smuggled out when a fellow prisoner was released in 1976.

Although the manuscript was not published while Mandela was in prison, he writes that "it forms the spine" of *Long Walk.* Thus, as a partial prison narrative, the book keeps company with other important works of literature composed behind bars: John Bunyan's *Pilgrim's Progress,* Antonio Gramsci's *Prison Notebooks,* Vaclav Havel's *The Power of the Powerless,* and Oscar Wilde's *De Profundis,* to name a few.

Although Mandela's choice of genre—the autobiography—was political rather than literary, *Long Walk to Freedom* nevertheless participates in a strong literary tradition. In the West, the first autobiography is generally considered to be the *Confessions* of Saint Augustine, written around A.D. 400. For centuries afterward, the biography or autobiography was used mainly as a form of religious testimony; John Bunyan, for example, titled his spiritual autobiography *Grace Abounding*. Beginning in the age of the Enlightenment, though, the purpose and tone of these genres shifted from the spiritual to the secular. Instead of the Christian hero, biographies and autobiographies began to feature an individual who had suffered and survived a personal crisis. In the nineteenth century, spiritual (although not necessarily religious) crises figured in Wordsworth's *The Prelude,* Tennyson's *In Memoriam,* and Cardinal Newman's *Apologia,* among others. Frederick Douglass—abolitionist, orator, reformer, and one-time slave—published his *Narrative of the Life of Frederick Douglass* (1845), telling of his journey to freedom, a combination of a physical, personal, and intellectual struggle. Like Mandela, Douglass wrote under extreme duress in a society besieged by racial conflict and ideological upheaval. When his *Narrative* was published, he feared his identity as a runaway slave would be revealed and fled to England.

Since Douglass, many political prisoners, refugees, and civil-rights activists have chosen to tell their stories through autobiography or other forms of personal narrative. In the mid-twentieth-century United States, both Martin Luther King, Jr., and Malcolm X—two civil rights leaders who espoused radically different courses of action—published autobiographical works. In *The Trumpet of Conscience* (1968), King calls for a nonviolent but aggressive revolution; likewise, *The Autobiography of Malcolm X* (1965) summarizes the author's more militant views on the fight for equal rights. Other important twentieth-century civil rights narratives include Ernesto Galarza's *Barrio Boy* (1971) and Eldridge Cleaver's *Soul on Ice* (1968).

South African contemporaries of Nelson Mandela have also produced personal accounts of the ongoing post-apartheid struggle to heal a wounded nation. In 1999 Desmond Tutu published his memoir, *No Future Without Forgiveness,* which details the Anglican archbishop's tenure as the chair of South Africa's Truth and Reconciliation Commission (established during Mandela's presidency). In the same year, Antjie Krog, a prominent South African journalist and poet, published *Country of My Skull: Guilt, Sorrow, and the Limits of Forgiveness in the New South Africa.* As the title suggests, this volume is an account of the difficulties faced by South Africa during its first post-apartheid years.

Critical Responses

When it first appeared in 1994, Mandela's autobiography was welcomed by readers and critics worldwide who were eager to learn more about the "Mosaic figure" who had led his South African people out of the bondage of apartheid. Although the book was published at the very beginning of Mandela's tenure as his country's first democratically elected president, Mandela's life, as a critic for *The New York Review of Books* notes, was already "mythologically complete." For this reason, the book is broadly appreciated as an introduction to the man—the mortal who resided behind the myth—

who writes with "candor about his own fears, vanities, blunders, and ambivalences." Similarly, a reviewer for *The New York Times* observes that,

> . . . like the hero in a Shakespearean drama, Mr. Mandela cannot help revealing himself: here are all the idiosyncrasies and complications that turned a man into a leader and that have at last turned that leader back into a man.
>
> —from *The New York Times*
> November 30, 1994
> Margo Jefferson

About the Book (cont.)

Appreciated for its revealing nature, the book is also praised for presenting a balanced self-portrait of a man who, almost paradoxically, combines "super-human patience, fortitude, and determination, as well as considerable self-deprecation." Indeed, Mandela's humility delights most readers, despite the fact that, as several critics point out, it occasionally leaves gaps in the text. For example, what Mandela calls Robben Island's "University," in which the prisoners taught one another various formal courses, was in fact known as "Mandela University." But most reviewers are quick to say that Mandela's modesty is neither a flaw nor a merely charming character trait; they recognize that his humility shapes his generous, forgiving brand of democracy—as one critic describes it, a "democracy grounded in his awareness of human frailty and courage. Always he sees the individual, whether friend or enemy."

Credit is often given as well to Richard Stengel, the *Time* magazine contributor with whom Mandela collaborated on the book, for having "preserved the unmistakable voice of Mr. Mandela—polite, good-humored—while curbing his tendency to speak in the collective voice of the movement." Another reviewer notes that "*Long Walk to Freedom* never reads like an as-told-to book. . . . With its memoir-like intimacy and its historical sweep, it sounds like Mandela."

The few criticisms that have been leveled at the book focus on Mandela's failure to tell the whole truth about some crucial events in his life. For example, Mandela gives only a brief, reductive account of his scandalous breakup with his second wife, Winnie. Although many critics respect Mandela for refusing to criticize his wife publicly, most would also agree with William Finnegan of the *New York Review of Books* that Winnie's behavior "was not merely a private matter . . . [her] growing thuggishness and lack of political discipline made her a pariah within the resistance" and ultimately "damage[d] . . . the integrity and credibility of the anti-apartheid movement." Finnegan concludes that, while Mandela's reticence "may be defensible in an autobiography, it distorts recent South African history." In a similar vein, critic Bill Keller notes that while Mandela repeatedly "defends the ANC's decision to take up arms," he also "glosses over the fact that what began as sabotage against electrical stations became for a time a campaign of terrorism against civilians."*

Reviewers of the book also detect in its final chapters a dwindling of narrative momentum. An otherwise complimentary review in *Publishers Weekly* notes that "This book—perhaps out of diplomacy and haste—covers the period since Mandela's 1990 release with less nuance and candor than other recent accounts"; likewise, a critic for *The New York Times* finds that the last fifty pages "whiz by in a blur of platitudes." Some believe this is because Mandela had less time for "lengthy reflection" in the closing chapters (whereas the first parts of the book were drafted in prison); others suggest that Mandela is perhaps "reluctant to say anything that might offend the former rivals who have become his partners in what is supposed to be a Government by consensus."

But these few minor criticisms of the book do nothing, in the view of most of Mandela's readers, to diminish its triumph as a portrait of both the man and the myth—"an uncanny combination of rebel, gentleman and patriot."

* From "The Practical Mr. Mandela" by Bill Keller from *The New York Times,* December 18, 1994. Copyright © 1994 by **The New York Times Company.**

The Book at a Glance

A **Book Review Worksheet** focusing on **plot and setting** appears on page 47 of this Study Guide.

A **Book Review Worksheet** focusing on **major characters** appears on page 46 of this Study Guide.

Plot and Setting

Long Walk to Freedom covers the life of Nelson Mandela from his birth in 1918 to his election as the first black president of South Africa in 1994. In the early chapters, Mandela focuses on the development of his political consciousness as a child and young man. He then traces his years as a college student, lawyer, and budding political activist. In the second half of the book Mandela recounts his arrest, conviction, imprisonment, and diplomatic efforts to end apartheid.

The book's setting is South Africa, a country with a troubled and racially divisive history. Mandela is torn between his love of South Africa and his hatred for what it has become in the hands of the white minority.

Structure and Point of View

The autobiography is organized chronologically. Mandela tells his story from the first-person point of view.

Major Characters

Nelson Mandela is the book's central character. Mandela is born into the Thembu tribe of the Xhosa nation, an identity he cherishes throughout his life. But after coming to see, as a young man, that black South Africans are oppressed at the hands of the white minority government, Mandela commits himself to the struggle for justice.

Oliver Tambo, Mandela's lifelong friend, works with Mandela, first as a law partner and later as a comrade in the struggle against apartheid.

Winnie Mandela, née Madikizela, is Nelson's second wife, whom he marries in 1958 shortly after divorcing Evelyn Mase. When Winnie is convicted in 1988 for her involvement in a kidnapping scandal, Nelson Mandela maintains her innocence. In 1992, however, the two separate.

F. W. de Klerk serves as South Africa's president from 1989 to 1994. He is a key figure in the negotiations to end apartheid, and in 1993 he is awarded the Nobel Peace Prize along with Mandela.

Themes

The development of a leader: Mandela highlights key moments in his formation as a leader, often pausing to reflect on the qualities of leadership that he admires and attempts to practice—optimism, dignity in the face of injustice, a deep understanding of the people one serves, and self-discipline, among others.

Difficult choices: Mandela is painfully aware of the personal sacrifices he has made in order to achieve a great good for a vast number of people. First as an outlaw and later as a prisoner, Mandela laments his inability to fulfill his roles as husband and father.

Belief in the fundamental goodness of humanity: Even during the darkest times, Mandela maintains faith in the human spirit. He claims never to hate his oppressors, only the system that produces racism and injustice.

The insidious nature of oppression: Mandela marvels at his youthful regard for the white man as a benefactor rather than oppressor.

A **Literary Elements Worksheet** that focuses on **theme** appears on page 51 of this Study Guide.

Major Symbols

Mandela himself comes to symbolize African nationalism and the struggle against apartheid. **Prison** becomes a symbol of the larger struggle against injustice. **Clothing** often functions symbolically as an expression of nationalism or power.

A **Literary Elements Worksheet** that focuses on **symbol** appears on page 50 of this Study Guide.

Rhetorical Devices

Anecdotes add texture and accessibility to the day-to-day life of an important political figure. Mandela also uses **appeals to emotion** to emphasize the psychic and physical pain he and others are forced to endure. Excerpts from Mandela's **speeches** provide examples of his rhetorical expertise.

A **Literary Elements Worksheet** focusing on **anecdotes** appears on page 49 of this Study Guide.

Foreshadowing

Mandela's frequent foreshadowing of the events leading up to his arrest and imprisonment adds suspense to the narrative.

A **Literary Elements Worksheet** that focuses on **foreshadowing** appears on page 48 of this Study Guide.

Figurative Language

The product of an oral tradition, Mandela is adept at using **similes and metaphors** to add shades of meaning and to clarify abstract concepts. The book's title itself depicts his life as a journey.

Options

Engaging Issues

The issues raised in Long Walk to Freedom *continue to be relevant and controversial today. This activity encourages students to grapple with these issues in ways relevant to their own lives.*

Use the following list of statements to introduce these issues. Have students read each statement, decide whether they agree or disagree, and then prepare a brief response explaining why. The response should contain at least one concrete example from their knowledge or experience.

When students are finished, they can gather in small groups to discuss their responses and attempt to reach a consensus. Alternatively, have students use the statements and responses to organize a debate.

STATEMENTS

Leadership Qualities

- A leader should be willing to lay down his or her life for a cause.
- It is okay for a leader to act secretly, without having sought advice or without making his or her plans known.
- It is more important for a leader to be practical-minded than it is for him or her to hold fast to ideals.
- A leader must have experienced some suffering or hardship in order to empathize with the less fortunate or the oppressed.

Group Identity

- It is okay for an oppressed group to use any means possible as it struggles for justice.
- The world would be a happier, more peaceful place if people thought of themselves first as human beings, and then as members of a particular nation or race.
- If a person belongs to a group that hurts or oppresses others, he or she should set an example by walking away from the group.

Difficult Choices

- If choosing to stand up for something I believe in would hurt several people close to me but help thousands of others, I would do it.
- The welfare of those we know and love should always be more important to us than the welfare of strangers.

FILM

Into Africa

Show a video recording of *Cry, the Beloved Country* (adapted from the novel by Alan Paton). Alternatively, show a travel video about South Africa or a documentary about the country's history. After students view the video, discuss with them what they have learned about South Africa and apartheid.

MAKING PERSONAL CONNECTIONS

A Walk of Your Own

Have students respond to one of the following prompts in their journals or Reader's Logs.

- Write about a time when you or someone you love was treated unfairly and you took action.
- Jot down several of your strongest beliefs. Then choose the one that is most important to you. Would you devote your life to this belief? Why or why not?

(Students should not have to share their entries with anyone else unless they choose to do so.)

READING AND LISTENING

Mandela Speaks

Listen to an audio recording of one of Nelson Mandela's speeches or have a student prepare a dramatic reading of one of them. Afterwards discuss the speech's content and/or rhetorical style.

Plot Synopsis and Literary Elements

Long Walk to Freedom

Section I: Chapters 1–15

Synopsis

Nelson Mandela is born in South Africa on July 18, 1918, the youngest son of a Thembu chief and a member of the Thembu royal household. Mandela passes the first part of his childhood in the small village of Qunu, where he lives happily with his mother (one of his father's three wives) and siblings. After his father's death, nine-year-old Nelson is sent to live with the Thembu king and is raised alongside the king's own son. There Mandela observes closely the regent and his court, learning basic principles of democratic governance. At the age of sixteen, Mandela participates in the circumcision ritual through which, in the Thembu tradition, a boy becomes a man.

Shortly thereafter, Mandela, who is to be trained as a counselor to the Thembu king, begins a course of studies at Clarkebury Institute, a Thembu college founded in 1825 by Methodist missionaries from England. After earning his junior certificate in two years—rather than the standard three—Mandela enrolls at Healdtown, a Wesleyan college, then the largest African school south of the equator. There, in the company of students from all over the country and continent, the young tribesman begins to think of himself in broader terms—not only as a Thembu, but as an African.

At the age of twenty-one, Mandela enters the university at Fort Hare. There he becomes active in campus politics while also developing an interest in world politics. For the first time, Mandela confronts the "dangerously radical" idea that the white people—both Dutch and English—had oppressed Africans while also trying to "civilize" them.

Before finishing his B.A. degree, Mandela flees with Justice, the king's son, to Johannesburg to escape marriages the king has arranged for them. There, Mandela begins to mingle with members of a multiracial organization called the African National Congress (ANC) whose goal is to establish equal rights for South Africans of all races.

In the early '40s, Mandela completes his B.A. degree by correspondence at the University of South Africa, and then his Bachelor of Law degree at the University of Witwatersrand. While working at a series of white law firms, Mandela grows increasingly committed to freeing Africans from white oppression. Between 1946 and 1947, Mandela marries and has two children, one of whom dies in infancy. He becomes a member of the ANC and is elected to the Executive Committee of the Transvaal branch of the organization. With other young ANC members he also helps found the Youth League, whose purposes are to broaden the ANC's appeal and to stage non-violent protests.

The 1948 general election strikes a hard blow to the ANC. It pits the United Party, which had supported Great Britain (and the Allies) in World War II, against the National Party, which had sympathized with Nazi Germany and whose main objectives are to free white South Africa from British influence and to further oppress black South Africans through a system known as *apartheid*. Daniel Malan, the National Party candidate, wins the election. He immediately passes several harsh apartheid laws that oust people of color from Parliament, make mixed marriages illegal, and dictate where people of different races can and cannot live.

In response to these laws, the ANC becomes an activist group. It establishes a program of action that uses civil disobedience, strikes, and boycotts as means of protest. Although he is skeptical of any action undertaken with other political groups, when the government passes the Suppression of Communism Act of 1950, outlawing any action taken to effect political change, Mandela finally concedes that cooperation with these groups is necessary. In alliance with the Communist Party and the South African Indian Congress, the ANC organizes a Day of Protest on which workers who belong to oppressed groups either stay home or do not open their businesses.

More apartheid laws are passed in 1952, further eroding black voters' rights and segregating them from whites. In response, the ANC devises a Campaign for the Defiance of Unjust Laws, under which volunteers deliberately invite arrest by breaking certain laws. When the government refuses to negotiate with the ANC, the campaign is launched. Over six months thousands of people participate, the ANC membership shoots up to 100,000, and the group receives enormous publicity.

Because of his anti-apartheid activities, Mandela is forced by the government to resign from the ANC and is forbidden to travel outside Johannesburg. In 1952, Mandela and another ANC member, Oliver Tambo, open a law firm dedicated to defending Africans accused of violating apartheid laws. During this period, Mandela begins advocating more violent means of protest, believing that the ANC's policy of nonviolence has become ineffective. In 1955 the ANC demands a new South African government. Along with many others, Mandela is arrested and charged with treason. Because the trial does not begin until 1959, the accused are not held in jail. During these difficult years, Mandela and his wife become estranged and divorce. Mandela soon meets and is married to Winnie Madikizela, with whom he will have two daughters.

Also during this period, a group of younger Africans who oppose the ANC's multiracial policy form the Pan Africanist Congress (PAC), dedicated to creating a purely African government. As protests escalate, the government declares a state of emergency and outlaws both the ANC and the PAC. In 1961, after the lengthy Treason Trial, Mandela and the others are found not guilty. With his law practice in ruins, Mandela commits himself to the underground life of a freedom fighter. Elusive and, in the eyes of the government, dangerous, Mandela becomes known as the "Black Pimpernel." He travels in disguise—often as a chauffeur—organizes and attends secret nighttime meetings, frequently changes his place of residence, and begins to campaign within the ANC for an armed struggle. After much internal dispute, the ANC authorizes Mandela to create a separate military organization that will allow the ANC itself to remain nonviolent.

Umkhonto we Sizwe (The Spear of the Nation), MK for short, is formed with Mandela, Joe Slovo, and Walter Sisulu in command. Mandela releases to the newspapers a statement demanding that the government hold a national conference to rewrite the constitution; if the government fails to comply, he implies, military action will be taken.

The MK settles on sabotage as its first method, since sabotage would inflict the least harm on people. On December 16, 1961—"Dingane's Day," the day white South Africans celebrate victory over black Africans—homemade bombs are set off at power plants and government offices in cities all over the country. Leaflets are released announcing the MK's existence and purpose, and, in response, the government steps up its counteroffensive.

That same month, the ANC receives an invitation from the Pan African Freedom Movement for East, Central, and Southern Africa (PAFMECSA) to attend its annual conference in February 1962. Mandela is chosen to lead the ANC's delegation to the conference. For the first time in his life, Mandela leaves South Africa and tours his native continent. After attending the conference in Ethiopia and there garnering support for the ANC's objectives, Mandela visits other African countries—Tunisia, Morocco, Mali, Guinea, Sierra Leone, Liberia, Ghana, and Senegal—to ask for their support. Although most countries agree to support the ANC, Mandela has to work hard to undo the ANC's negative image: because of rumors spread by the PAC, the ANC is widely believed to be a Communist organization.

After a brief visit to London and eight weeks of military training in Ethiopia, Mandela is called back to

South Africa by the ANC. Once home, Mandela alerts his ANC colleagues to the organization's negative reputation and urges them to consider restructuring the ANC's alliance with other groups so that the ANC is, at least on the surface, the leader. Driving back to Johannesburg from a meeting with the ANC's chief, Mandela is pulled over by the police and arrested. He refuses bail and, having decided to represent himself at trial, begins spending his solitary time in jail preparing his case. Members of the ANC propose an escape plan, but Mandela denounces the plan as premature and proposes trying again later.

Literary Elements

Themes: As Mandela tells the story of his youth, he pays special attention to the people and experiences that help shape his attitudes about **leadership** and **democracy.** As a child playing with other boys in the veld, Mandela learns to defeat his "opponents without dishonoring them," and from his father, a Thembu chief, he inherits a "proud rebelliousness, a stubborn sense of fairness." Later, in the court of his guardian, the king, Mandela learns that in a true democracy all people can speak and be heard. As a student, Mandela develops self-discipline and, through student politics, experiences the "sense of power that comes from having right and justice on one's side." During his young manhood, Mandela's horizons broaden and his consciousness is raised. He begins to think of himself as a South African rather than a Thembu and begins to understand the **insidious nature of the oppression** he and other black South Africans have suffered at the hands of the white minority rulers: In the name of "civilization," European colonizers had created a racist society in which the oppressed members felt grateful rather than angry. Once fully aware of these unjust conditions, Mandela commits himself to a life of **difficult choices.** Through the failure of his law practice and first marriage, his life as an underground freedom fighter, and ultimately his arrest and conviction, Mandela learns painful lessons about sacrificing one's private life and even one's freedom for a greater cause.

Symbols

- Before his first day of school, Mandela's father gives him a pair of his own cutoff trousers and cinches them around the small boy's waist; Mandela is fiercely proud to be wearing "proper" attire rather than tribal dress. Later, before Mandela enters Fort Hare, the regent gives him his first double-breasted suit, which makes Mandela feel "grown-up and sophisticated." These items of **clothing,** symbolic of the western civilization Mandela will soon learn to question, contrast with the native dress Mandela later wears as a defendant in the "white man's court."

- While listening to the poet Mqhayi speak at Healdtown, Mandela becomes aware of the **spear** as a symbol of Africa's inevitable "victory over the interloper." The spear later resurfaces in Umkhonto we Sizwe—the Spear of the Nation, the military group Mandela helps to found.

- During his first imprisonment at Rivonia, where his friend Walter Sisulu is also incarcerated, the two decide that Walter should apply for bail while **Mandela,** who had "become a public symbol of rebellion and struggle," should not. This is Mandela's first recognition of himself as a cultural icon and of the power he wields as such.

Figurative Language: To describe his strong tribal identity as a youth, Mandela uses the following **simile:** "I was like a boy who worships a local soccer hero and is not interested in a national soccer star with whom he has no connection." In addition to cultural imagery, Mandela frequently uses **natural images**—drawn, no doubt, from his boyhood roaming the veld—to describe key moments in his life. For example, he writes that on first viewing the grand home of the king, where he went to live after his father's death, he "felt like a sapling pulled root and branch from the earth and flung into the center of a stream"; in this new, heady environment he learns that "a leader . . . is like a shepherd. He stays behind the flock, letting the most nimble go out ahead, whereupon the others follow, not realizing that all along they are being directed from behind." Later, Mandela muses that the experience of listening to the poet Mqhayi "was like [watching] a comet streaking across the night sky."

Plot: Mandela organizes the story of his youth around certain turning points that carry him from one level of awareness to the next. The first such moment comes when he gazes on his new home, that of the Thembu regent: "Until then . . . I had no thought of money, or class, or fame, or power. Suddenly a new world opened before me. . . . I felt many of my established beliefs and loyalties begin to ebb away." The next major turning point is his circumcision, a Thembu boy's ritual entry into manhood, after which he listens to a chief speak of the oppression of black South Africans by whites. The chief, he writes, "had planted a seed, and though I let that seed lie dormant for a long season, it eventually began to grow." His exposure to the poet Mqhayi constitutes another turning point as he wavers between "pride in myself as a Xhosa and a feeling of kinship with other Africans." Mandela's departure from Fort Hare without a degree marks his first serious rebellion against authority and moves him firmly into the realm of political activism. At this point the story's **suspense** heightens as Mandela's political activities intensify and he embarks first upon the life of a fugitive and then that of a militant freedom fighter. (See **foreshadowing,** below.) With his arrest and imprisonment, one level of suspense is resolved while another begins to form: What will Mandela's life behind bars hold for both the man and the movement?

Foreshadowing: Perhaps because the ultimate outcome of his story—his election to the presidency of South Africa—is well known, Mandela makes every effort to inject his narrative with suspense, often through the device of foreshadowing. During his early years in the struggle, for example, Mandela spends much of his time away from his home and children. "I missed them a great deal during those days," he writes, "long before I had any inkling that I would spend decades apart from them." Likewise, mere days before his arrest, the Working Committee of the ANC urges Mandela to make a personal visit to Chief Luthuli. One member objects, worried about Mandela's safety, but, Mandela recalls, "this wise advice was overruled by everyone, including myself." These comments—and many others like them—subtly build the reader's uncomfortable anticipation of the trials to come.

Rhetorical Devices: The **rhetorical patterns** that structure many of Mandela's public statements (such as letters and speeches) reflect the leader's philosophy and his great sense of responsibility to his people. For example, in a letter written from underground and printed in African newspapers on Freedom Day, Mandela refuses to turn himself in, stating instead that "I have chosen this course which is more difficult and which entails more risk and hardship. . . . I have had to separate myself from my dear wife and children. . . . I have had to close my business. . . . I shall fight the Government side by side with you. . . ." This series of parallel statements, each beginning with the emphatic "I," is then followed by a shift in focus to his audience: "What are you going to do?" Such rhetorical patterns emphasize Mandela's deep personal commitment to the cause as well as his sense of kinship with other black Africans and his desire to energize and mobilize his people. He concludes the letter by asserting that "the struggle is my life": Mandela is and will continue to be absolutely identified with the cause he has chosen.

Mandela also uses humorous **anecdotes** and **emotional appeals** to add depth to his story. For example, Mandela wryly relates how he approached the home of a priest for a clandestine meeting, wearing a shabby disguise which succeeded all too well. The woman who answered the door took him to be a vagrant and slammed the door in his face. Such humor, though, is punctuated by pathos, as when Mandela's five-year-old son asks his mother, "Where does Daddy live?"

Section II: Chapters 16–38

Synopsis

In late 1962, Mandela stands trial for leaving the country illegally and for inciting African workers to strike. Knowing that he is guilty of these "crimes," Mandela decides to use this high-profile opportunity to put the state itself on trial. After the prosecution produces more than a hundred witnesses to testify to Mandela's crimes, Mandela surprises the court by calling no witnesses but instead making a lengthy and eloquent statement of his beliefs—in the native democracy of African culture; in the human spirit, which must protest against injustice; and in his own innocence and the government's guilt. In spite of Mandela's powerful message and pledges of support from governments around the world, he is found guilty and sentenced to five years in prison.

Mandela is first held in Pretoria Local, along with other political prisoners from the ANC and the PAC. During late 1961 and early 1962, the government passes another series of apartheid laws, including the Ninety-Day Detention Law, which allows the police to arrest without a warrant anyone suspected of a political crime, and the Sabotage Act, which allows for house arrests. In May 1962 Mandela and three other prisoners are moved to Robben Island, off the southwestern coast of South Africa. Under harsh and demeaning conditions, Mandela refuses to surrender his dignity, challenging any guard or official who acts outside the law.

After several months Mandela is taken back to Pretoria, where he discovers that the police have raided a meeting of the MK High Command at Liliesleaf Farm in Rivonia and arrested a dozen men in one fell swoop. Mandela and the others are charged with sabotage and conspiracy with intent to overthrow the government, for which the supreme penalty is death. Over the course of three months, the state produces a mass of evidence against the defendants—including a six-page Plan of Action confiscated during the

raid. Although the state contends that this document, which contains plans for the initiation of guerilla warfare, has been approved and adopted by the ANC, the defense contends that the document is unapproved and, given Mandela's criticisms of it, would have remained so. The defense opens with a statement given by Mandela that makes several points: It explains in detail the ANC's historical policy of nonviolence and its ongoing attempt to avoid civil war; reiterates the ANC's commitment to nonracial democracy; condemns the indignities imposed on Africans by whites; and asserts Mandela's readiness to die for his beliefs. Almost a year after the trial begins, all the main defendants are found guilty and sentenced to life in prison.

First at Pretoria Local and then again at Robben Island, Mandela begins serving his sentence. Living conditions in the prison are harsh: The cells are cold and damp; clothes are threadbare and inappropriate; and food consists mainly of thin, boiled mealies (corn). The political prisoners in Mandela's section spend their days laboring—first pounding large pieces of rock into gravel and later mining lime at a nearby quarry. From the beginning, Mandela considers it his personal challenge someday to emerge from prison with an undiminished spirit. To this end, he views his struggle inside the prison walls as a microcosm of the larger struggle for freedom he and his people are waging on the outside.

Periodically, visitors from the outside—journalists, advocates, politicians—come to inspect prison conditions. Before these visits, prison authorities typically make modest attempts to improve conditions. But Mandela, the spokesman for his group, always speaks calmly, candidly, and at great length to these visitors about the appalling treatment he and his colleagues are receiving. Sometimes these sessions yield improvements, such as desks and stools for studying; other times they do not.

At first, Mandela is allowed only one thirty-minute visit, one outgoing letter, and one incoming letter every six months. Even so, mail is often withheld or heavily censored, and the few visits he has from Winnie are strictly monitored. Mandela and the others are permitted to study for diplomas or degrees, but many of the books required for certain courses are banned or withheld by the authorities. Newspapers—totally forbidden—are valued above all else, and Mandela and his companions devise elaborate ways to circulate smuggled news. Once discovered in possession of a newspaper, Mandela serves three days in isolation without food.

A variety of methods are used to fight injustice in prison. The prisoners sometimes attempt to develop friendships with warders and, over time, communicate to them the philosophy and beliefs of the ANC. The prisoners often refuse to perform undignified tasks such as carrying the warders' lunchboxes, and occasionally they go on hunger strikes or organize other group protests.

To pass time at the quarry and on weekends, the men engage in long debates about politics and other topics. By 1966 the guards at the quarry have adopted rather lax attitudes and often allow the men to talk without interruption. But in September 1966 the prime minister of South Africa is assassinated, and prison conditions once again become harsh and unforgiving.

On the outside, the South African government grows stronger while other African nations, such as Rhodesia (now Zimbabwe), struggle successfully against imperialism. Mandela feels that if the ANC's struggle is ever to succeed, the ANC and the PAC will have to reconcile, and so he works diligently to unite prisoners from both groups. The PAC, however, remains hostile to the ANC.

In 1968–69 Mandela suffers several personal hardships: First, he receives word that his mother has died and is denied permission to attend her funeral; shortly thereafter he learns that Winnie has been arrested, imprisoned, brutally interrogated, and eventually charged with attempting to revive the ANC; and finally he is informed that his oldest son has been killed in a car wreck. Mandela, overcome with grief, is comforted by his close friend Walter Sisulu.

Although small victories are hard won and slow to come, by 1969 conditions in prison have considerably improved. The prisoners are clothed in more appropriate attire, attend Sunday religious services, play board games on weekends, and, during the Christmas season, prepare and perform a concert and a play. In 1970, though, a new commanding officer arrives and reverses these changes: Privileges such as studying are revoked, cells are raided, and young, brutal guards harass and demoralize the men. When three Supreme Court justices visit, Mandela enumerates the prisoners' complaints in front of the commandant himself, who, provoked, becomes angry and aggressive. Several months later the new commandant is dismissed.

Literary Elements

Themes: Almost ironically, the theme of the **fundamental goodness of humanity** stands out sharply in Part II against the dismal backdrop of Mandela's imprisonment. During his final statement at the Rivonia trial, Mandela asserts that "Men . . . are not capable of doing nothing, of saying nothing, . . . of not protesting against oppression, of not striving for the good society and the good life. . . ." His belief in humanity's essential goodness extends even to the warders who have almost exclusive control over the prisoners' day-to-day lives. "I always tried to be decent to the warders in my section," Mandela writes. "It was ANC policy to try to educate all people, even our enemies: we believed that all men, even prison service warders, were capable of change." Likewise, after the brutal commanding officer Badenhorst is dismissed, he approaches Mandela and wishes him good luck. Mandela reflects that this "was a useful reminder that all men, even the most seemingly cold-blooded, have a core of decency. . . . Ultimately, Badenhorst was not evil; his inhumanity had been foisted upon him by an inhuman system." By maintaining his belief in the evils of the system—not of individuals—Mandela avoids falling into the trap of hatred, which in turn would have corrupted his own inner strength. Indeed, by remaining constantly aware of the **insidious nature of oppression,** Mandela himself is able to transcend it.

From the Rivonia trial onward, Mandela's central **difficult choice** is to preserve his inner core of strength rather than surrender to despair. While on trial, Mandela and his colleagues face the supreme penalty: death. Rather than devise ways to escape or lessen this penalty—such as pleading guilty or, in the event of the sentence, arranging for an appeal—they face death squarely and remind themselves that "if anything we might serve the cause greater in death as martyrs than we ever could in life." Once in prison, Mandela chooses consistently to take the high road of dignity and self-respect rather than the low road of anger and hostility. The prisoner's most difficult challenge, as he puts it, is "how to emerge from prison undiminished, how to conserve and even replenish one's beliefs." Somehow, perhaps aware of his own responsibility to those who regard him as the symbol of the movement, Mandela manages to do just this.

His ability to transcend the injustices of his situation attests to Mandela's ongoing **growth as a leader.** His willingness to die for his cause; his ability to "put up a bold front despite what one feels inside"; his undying optimism and self-respect—these qualities both enable him to survive under the most potentially damaging circumstances and signify the character of a man who will someday lead his nation out of bondage.

Symbols

Clothing continues to symbolize identity, resistance to oppression, and oppression itself.

- On the first day of his trial, after being arrested and charged with illegal exit from the country, Mandela enters the courtroom wearing a Xhosa leopard-skin kaross rather than a suit. "I had chosen traditional dress," he writes, "to emphasize the symbolism that I was a black African walking into a white man's court." Mandela's dress also symbolizes the power of self-definition and pinpoints the source of his oppressor's fears.

- Once in prison, Mandela reports that Africans are given short trousers as a symbol of their status as "boys." Here, clothing symbolizes an identity forced on a group of oppressed people by its oppressors. Mandela, who recognizes and abhors this symbolism, vigorously protests this attire and, within three years, all African prisoners are given long pants.

- After his son Thembi dies, Mandela recalls a day when the boy approached him wearing one of Mandela's old jackets and announced that he would look after the family during his father's absence. Mandela realizes that "he must have taken some comfort and pride in wearing his father's clothing, just as I once did with my own father's." Here, as in Part I when the young Mandela is given various "grown-up" clothes, clothing symbolizes the self one is striving to become, the identity one longs to assume.

- Another motif running throughout Part II is **prison as a symbol of a larger unjust society:** "We regarded the struggle in prison as a microcosm of the struggle as a whole." This conceptual link between the inside and the outside gives Mandela and his comrades a sense of purpose and focus, and thus plays a practical as well as symbolic role.

- **Mandela** himself continues to symbolize the struggle of the African against the oppressors: On his first day of trial, wearing tribal garb, he feels himself "to be the embodiment of African nationalism, the inheritor of Africa's difficult but noble past and her uncertain future."

Descriptive Language: To convey the bleakness of his surroundings in prison Mandela often uses **language that appeals to the senses.** "The cells had been constructed hurriedly, and the walls were perpetually damp," he writes of the facilities on Robben Island. "When I lay down, I could feel the wall with my feet and my head grazed the concrete at the other side." Such language is also used to describe work conditions at the quarry—"Even in the sun, I shivered in my light khaki shirt"—the loathsome diet the prisoners are served, and the challenges of cleaning oneself with icy saltwater.

Rhetorical Devices: Mandela aptly depicts the emotional extremes of prison life by using both **humor** and **pathos.** The reader is amused by **anecdotes** of the thick-headed "Suitcase" or appalled at the story of the prisoner who steals a newspaper from the preacher's briefcase during prayer, resulting in the prisoners being forced out of bed to stand naked for an hour in the dark, bitterly cold courtyard while their cells are searched.

Even though he is generally hesitant to discuss his private emotions, Mandela relates, with great pain, a series of devastating events that occurred in 1968–69. He is comforted by his friend Walter, who "said nothing, but only held my hand. I do not know how long he remained with me. There is nothing that one man can say to another at such a time." For Mandela, the failure of words often signifies the deepest of emotions.

Characterization: "The most important person in any prisoner's life is. . . the warder in one's section," Mandela writes. To convey this, he often goes to great lengths to depict a particular warder. For example, the warder flown in to help implement a crackdown is described using both **direct** and **indirect characterization.** "Van Rensburg was a big, clumsy, brutish fellow who did not speak but shouted," Mandela reports. He then goes on to complete the portrait by relating the character's words and actions: During one of the prisoners' debates at the quarry, Van Rensburg "marched over and bellowed at us in English, a language in which he was not expert, 'You talk too much, but you work too few!'"

Allusion: Mandela refers on occasion to Western literature or literary figures—Shakespeare, Sophocles' *Antigone,* and later, in Part III, John Steinbeck's *The Grapes of Wrath* and Leo Tolstoy's *War and Peace.* Such references signify Mandela's basic points of reference as a product of a fundamentally Western culture. But they also make a more subtle statement about using the tools of the oppressor in an attempt to defeat the oppressor.

Section III: Chapters 39–76

Synopsis

There is an influx of political prisoners to Robben Island in 1971–72, many of them MK (the Spear of the Nation) soldiers who are militant and uncooperative. Mandela is often called upon to mediate between these men and the prison officials.

Mandela's group begins collecting seaweed at the seashore, which is a pleasant diversion. They also continue to study and, over time, organize their own "university," in which they teach one another courses based on their own areas of expertise.

In 1974, Mandela and three others plan an escape from a dentist's office in Cape Town, where they have requested appointments. They find, though, that their plan has been anticipated, so they abandon it.

At the encouragement of the others, Mandela secretly begins to write his memoirs. When a draft is finished and has been transcribed into shorthand and smuggled out of the prison, Mandela and his fellow inmates bury the original manuscript in the courtyard

Plot Synopsis and Literary Elements (cont.)

Long Walk to Freedom

garden. It is soon discovered, and the prisoners' study privileges are suspended.

In 1976, the minister of prisons visits Mandela and makes him an offer: If Mandela will recognize the legitimacy of the Transkei government—one of several quasi-independent homelands set up by the government to quell African nationalism—Mandela's sentence will be reduced and he will be allowed to move to the Transkei. Mandela rejects the offer and expresses his disapproval of the policy.

The mid-1970s see a rekindling of the spirit of protest that had all but died out in the '60s. Mandela is struck by how conservative he and his colleagues must seem to the young, impatient protesters, many of whom reject the ANC. He goes to great lengths to educate those younger activists he meets in prison and encourages them to be disciplined and to strive for unity above all else.

By the end of the decade, Mandela's group is relieved of their manual labor duties. Mandela spends his time gardening, exercising, and reading novels. The group is also allowed to watch films, and their diet improves. In 1980, they are given the right to buy newspapers. The papers are heavily censored, but the group still manages to discover through other sources that the ANC has launched a "Free Mandela" campaign and has stepped up its sabotage. The government responds by militarizing the country.

Life continues to be difficult for Winnie, a popular figure among the young radicals. She is imprisoned repeatedly and finally banished to a small township in a remote area.

Without warning, Mandela and three others are transferred in 1982 to Pollsmoor prison on the mainland near Cape Town. Their accommodations there are luxurious compared to those on the island. Meanwhile, the struggle intensifies on the outside, and casualties on both sides increase. The government again offers Mandela his freedom in 1985, on the condition that the ANC put down its arms. In a speech read by his daughter at a rally, Mandela

rejects the offer, puts the onus of violence back on the government, and insists that freedom from prison is not freedom from apartheid.

Soon Mandela enters into a series of secret talks with the minister of justice, Kobie Coetsee. In these infrequent conversations, Mandela insists on the distinction between the ANC and the Communist Party and reiterates the ANC's commitment to negotiation, not violence. Coetsee eventually proposes another series of meetings between Mandela and a committee of senior government officials. Mandela discusses this proposition with his colleagues, who have mixed responses but support his decision to go ahead with the talks. Mandela uses the meetings to educate the government about the ANC; to advance the idea that the government should represent all people—one person, one vote; and to demand that the government demilitarize before the ANC does.

After being hospitalized with tuberculosis for six weeks in 1987–88, Mandela is released to a private house on the grounds of Pollsmoor prison. There he lives in near freedom, enjoying a private cook and frequent visits from friends and family. With his colleagues he writes and sends a memo in March 1989 to President Botha requesting negotiations. A visit with Botha is finally granted in July; shortly thereafter Botha resigns and F. W. de Klerk is elected. Mandela sees de Klerk as a pragmatist and hopes the tide will turn.

De Klerk, at the urging of Mandela, releases many of Mandela's colleagues under no bans, ensuring disciplined behavior from them, and begins to dismantle some aspects of apartheid. Mandela writes to de Klerk and requests a series of negotiations between the government and the ANC. At a meeting with de Klerk, Mandela asks that the ban on the ANC be lifted and that all political prisoners be released. In February 1990 the president lifts bans on the ANC and other protest groups and, eight days later, releases Mandela from prison.

Life as a free man is chaotic and demanding for Mandela. Violence and poverty are extreme in many areas of the nation, and Mandela repeatedly begs his followers to live peacefully and to love all people, even whites, but to hate and reform the system.

A group of Zulus who are members of the Inkatha Freedom Party effectively declares war on the ANC and turns the state of Natal into a killing ground. When acts of extreme violence go unpunished, the ANC suspects that the Inkathas are being backed by the government in an attempt to divide Africans from one another and forestall negotiations.

Talks between the ANC and the government begin. De Klerk, nervous about majority rule, wants to set up a system of "group rights" whereby whites maintain a minority veto. Mandela rejects this as apartheid in disguise and insists on a new constitution and, in the meantime, an interim government.

Mandela travels to his homeland and visits his mother's grave near Qunu; he returns to Robben Island to encourage prisoners to accept the government's offer of release; and he visits several Western nations, including the United States, to call for continued sanctions. Back home in July 1990, he finds that violence has escalated. In August the ANC and the government sign an agreement to suspend arms. Still, Inkatha violence in Natal continues, unhampered by government interference, and when de Klerk remains silent on the issue, the ANC suspends negotiations in May 1991.

Not until September 1992 do Mandela and de Klerk sign a Record of Understanding. By February of 1993 the two parties agree to a new government of proportional representation, a multiparty cabinet, a transitional executive council, and elections by the end of the year.

Mandela experiences extreme highs and lows in his personal life during this period. He and Winnie, estranged by many years apart and by the stress of the struggle, agree to separate, and Mandela's closest friend and colleague, Oliver Tambo, dies of a stroke soon thereafter. In 1993 Mandela and de Klerk are jointly awarded the Nobel Peace Prize. Mandela is

deeply moved.

General elections take place in April 1994. The ANC wins by slightly less than the two-thirds margin that would give it the right to create a new constitution independently. Mandela is inaugurated on May 10, 1994, proud of the many miles he and the ANC have walked but still conscious of the long road that lies ahead.

Literary Elements

Themes: Mandela's **development as a leader** and as a diplomat comes to fruition in the final years of his imprisonment and in the years that follow his release. As the struggle intensifies on the outside and sends an influx of young, radical, confrontational prisoners to Robben Island, Mandela honors their points of view but also encourages them to put unity before all else. And in later years, as a key player in the negotiations to end apartheid, Mandela continues to apply lessons learned in his youth—defeating one's opponents without dishonoring them, for example—and to exercise skills he has honed as a freedom fighter and political prisoner—patience, self-discipline, compromise, persistence, and selflessness. As Mandela reflects near the end of the book—in a tribute to fellow participants in the struggle—apartheid was deeply wounding, but it "had another, unintended effect, and that was that it produced . . . men of such extraordinary courage, wisdom, and generosity that their like may never be known again." The same, of course, could be said of Mandela himself.

Mandela also reflects late in the book on the most **painful choice** his life has required of him—the choice to put the welfare of many anonymous people before the welfare of those he knows and loves intimately. Although he takes responsibility for this choice, he insists (as he does in the Rivonia trial) that the true culprit is oppression itself: "In South Africa, a man who tried to fulfill his duty to his people was inevitably ripped from his family and his home. . . ."

Other difficult choices Mandela must make in later

years include the decision to begin negotiations without the knowledge or counsel of his comrades; the decision to refuse to accept the government's offer of a conditional release from prison; and the series of decisions he must make regarding the negotiations themselves—for example, when to suspend the armed struggle so as to allow negotiations to move forward.

Throughout the negotiations, Mandela's opponents fear that minority rule will mean the oppression, in turn, of white South Africans. Mandela strives to reassure them that, according to his vision, the new government will be based on the fundamental principles of democracy and justice for all. As he advances these ideas, we see Mandela's **belief in the goodness of humanity** come into play in the political arena.

Figurative Language: Mandela continues to use a variety of metaphors, **similes,** and **symbols** in his writing.

- At the coast, Mandela and his fellow prisoners "laughed at the colony of penguins, which resembled a brigade of clumsy, flat-footed soldiers."
- Mandela's return to gardening—a love born in his youth—functions symbolically as the leader-gardener manages to create beauty even in the ugliest of environments.
- When speculating as to why he and the others were removed from Robben Island, Mandela notes that the island "was becoming a sustaining myth in the struggle, and they wanted to rob it of some of its symbolic import by removing us."
- Mandela refers to his cottage at Victor Verster prison as a "gilded cage."
- In a reflection on his good friend Oliver Tambo, Mandela alludes to Plato's allegory of the metals in which people are classified as gold, silver, and lead: "Oliver was pure gold. . . ."
- In the book's poetic closing pages, several resonating images are used: "Man's goodness is a flame that can be hidden but never extinguished"; "the chains on any one of my people were the chains on all of them, the chains on all of my people were

the chains on me"; and, in an explicit reference to the book's title metaphor, "We have not taken the final step of our journey, but the first step on a longer and even more difficult road."

Rhetorical Devices: Mandela continues to use **humor** as a tonic to the extreme seriousness of his story. Readers are relieved and amused, for example, when the head of the prison discovers the prisoners' seafood stew, which they boiled up in a large drum, and responds by sampling the fare and deeming it "tasty." Mandela is not afraid to poke fun at himself. The story of how the prison cook circumvents Mandela's preference for cheap Nederburg wine by letting the dinner guests choose their wine entertains readers while also showing that this great political thinker is in many ways disarmingly naïve. Another light moment occurs when he instructs voters to place a check mark on the ballot next to "the face of a young and handsome man." Such moments are welcome reminders of Mandela's humanity and ordinariness.

Emotionally charged moments also help readers see the man behind the myth. His first "noncontact visits"—with his daughter and granddaughter, and then with Winnie—are "dizzying experience[s]," full of "profound joy."

Style: Perhaps because he is self-conscious about the historical role he has played, Mandela's style in the chapters describing the negotiations is less fluid and self-revealing than earlier chapters. In the book's final pages, though, Mandela returns to a more introspective, philosophical voice as he meditates on the distances he has traveled and the long walk still to come. Additionally, Mandela's return to his homeland—both in person and, at the book's conclusion, in his thoughts—gives closure to the book's **narrative structure.**

Reader's Log: Model

Reading actively   In your reader's log you record your ideas, questions, comments, interpretations, guesses, predictions, reflections, challenges—any responses you have to the books you are reading.

Keep your reader's log with you while you are reading. You can stop at any time to write. You may want to pause several times during your reading time to capture your thoughts while they are fresh in your mind, or you may want to read without interruption and write when you come to a stopping point such as the end of a chapter or the end of the book.

Each entry you make in your reader's log should include the date, the title of the book you are reading, and the pages you have read since your last entry (pages ____ to ____).

Example

Sept. 21

<u>Fahrenheit 451</u>

pages 3 to 68

This book reminds me a lot of another book we read in class last year, <u>1984</u> by George Orwell. They're both books about the future—<u>1984</u> was written in the 1940s so it was the future then—a bad future where the government is very repressive and you can be arrested for what you think, say, or read. They're also both about a man and a woman who try to go against the system together. <u>Fahrenheit 451</u> is supposed to be about book censorship, but I don't think it's just about that—I think it's also about people losing their brain power by watching TV all the time and not thinking for themselves. <u>1984</u> did not have a very happy ending, and I have a feeling this book isn't going to either.

Exchanging ideas   Exchange reader's logs with a classmate and respond in writing to each other's most recent entries. (Your entries can be about the same book or different ones.) You might ask a question, make a comment, give your own opinion, recommend another book—in other words, discuss anything that's relevant to what you are reading.

Or: Ask your teacher, a family member, or a friend to read your most recent entries and write a reply to you in your reader's log.

Or: With your teacher's guidance, find an online pen pal in another town, state, or country and have a continuing book dialogue by e-mail.

Reader's Log: Starters

When I started reading this book, I thought . . .

I changed my mind about . . . because . . .

My favorite part of the book was . . .

My favorite character was . . . because . . .

I was surprised when . . .

I predict that . . .

I liked the way the writer . . .

I didn't like . . . because . . .

This book reminded me of . . .

I would (wouldn't) recommend this book to a friend because . . .

This book made me feel . . .

This book made me think . . .

This book made me realize . . .

While I was reading I pictured . . . (Draw or write your response.)

The most important thing about this book is . . .

If I were (name of character), I would (wouldn't) have . . .

What happened in this book was very realistic (unrealistic) because . . .

My least favorite character was . . . because . . .

I admire (name of character) for . . .

One thing I've noticed about the author's style is . . .

If I could be any character in this book, I would be . . . because . . .

I agree (disagree) with the writer about . . .

I think the title is a good (strange/misleading) choice because . . .

A better title for this book would be . . . because . . .

In my opinion, the most important word (sentence/paragraph) in this book is . . . because . . .

(Name of character) reminds me of myself because . . .

(Name of character) reminds me of somebody I know because . . .

If I could talk to (name of character), I would say . . .

When I finished this book, I still wondered . . .

This book was similar to (different from) other books I've read because it . . .

This book was similar to (different from) other books by this writer because it . . .

I think the main thing the writer was trying to say was . . .

This book was better (worse) than the movie version because . . .

(Event in book) reminded me of (something that happened to me) when . . .

Double-Entry Journal: Models

Responding to the text Draw a line down the middle of a page in your reader's log. On the left side, copy a meaningful passage from the book you're reading—perhaps a bit of dialogue, a description, or a character's thought. (Be sure to note the number of the page you copied it from—you or somebody else may want to find it later.) On the right side, write your response to the quotation. Why did you choose it? Did it puzzle you? confuse you? strike a chord? What does it mean to you?

Example

Quotation	Response
"It is a truth universally acknowledged, that a single man in possession of a good fortune must be in want of a wife." (page 1)	This is the first sentence of the book. When I first read it I thought the writer was serious—it seemed like something people might have believed when it was written. Soon I realized she was making fun of that attitude. I saw the movie Pride and Prejudice, but it didn't have a lot of funny parts, so I didn't expect the book to be funny at all. It is though, but not in an obvious way.

Creating a dialogue journal Draw a line down the middle of a page in your reader's log. On the left side, comment on the book you're reading—the plot so far, your opinion of the characters, or specifics about the style in which the book is written. On the right side of the page, your teacher or a classmate will provide a response to your comments. Together you create an ongoing dialogue about the novel as you are reading it.

Example

Your Comment	Response
The Bennet girls really seem incredibly silly. They seem to care only about getting married to someone rich or going to balls. That is all their parents discuss, too. The one who isn't like that, Mary, isn't realistic either, though. And why doesn't anyone work?!	I wasn't really bothered by their discussion of marriage and balls. I expected it because I saw the movie Emma, and it was like this, too. What I don't understand is why the parents call each other "Mr." and "Mrs."—everything is so formal. I don't think women of that class were supposed to work back then. And people never really work on TV shows or in the movies or in other books, do they?

Name _____ Date _____

Group Discussion Log

Group members

....

....

....

....

Book discussed

Title: ....

Author: ....

Pages _____ to _____

Three interesting things said by members of the group

....

....

....

....

....

....

....

....

What we did well today as a group

....

....

....

What we could improve

....

....

....

....

Our next discussion will be on _____. We will discuss pages _____to _____.

Glossary and Vocabulary

- **Vocabulary Words** are preceded by an asterisk (*) and may appear in the Vocabulary Worksheets.
- Words are listed in their order of appearance.
- The definition and the part of speech are based on the way the word is used in the book. For other uses of the word, check a dictionary.

Section I: Chapters 1–15
Chapter 1

*colloquial *adj.:* informal; having to do with the words or phrases characteristic of informal speech

*venerable *adj.:* worthy of respect by virtue of age, dignity, or position

patrilineal *adj.:* designating descent or kinship through the father rather than the mother

euphonious *adj.:* the quality of having a pleasant sound

*misnomer *n.:* a wrong name for a person or thing

straitened *adj.:* lacking sufficient money

Chapter 2

ocher *n.:* an earthy clay of yellow or reddish-brown color

*emulation *n.:* the act of imitation, especially of a person one admires

*assimilated *v.:* incorporated into one's thinking; absorbed

*axiom *n.:* a statement that is accepted as true

*proselytizing *n.:* the act of trying to convert a person to one's beliefs

Chapter 3

coterie *n.:* a clique; a group of people who share common interests or ideas

*succinctly *adv.:* in a clear and brief manner

*cogently *adv.:* in a forceful and compelling way; persuasively

*propitious *adj.:* favorable; advantageous

panegyric *n.:* a formal speech praising a person

*idiom *n.:* the language or dialect of a particular people, region, etc.

Chapter 4

stoicism *n.:* indifference to pleasure or pain

Chapter 5

*obsequiously *adv.:* in a fawning manner; showing too great a desire to obey or please

*deference *n.:* courteous regard or respect

*taciturn *adj.:* uncommunicative; generally silent

Chapter 6

encroachment *n.:* advancement or intrusion, especially in a gradual way

verdant *adj.:* green

*desultory *adj.:* in a random manner; not methodical

*indigenous *adj.:* existing naturally in a region or country

Chapter 7

*platitudes *n.:* clichés; common or trite remarks

*capitulate *v.:* to surrender; to stop resisting

Chapter 8

de facto: existing in fact but not by legal or official establishment

de jure: existing by legal or official establishment

cosmology *n.:* the study of the origin and form of the universe; here used to mean the perceived natural order

*volition *n.:* the act of making a deliberate and conscious choice

*pernicious *adj.:* destructive; causing great ruin

*arbiter *n.:* judge

*remonstrated *v.:* said in protest or objection

stalwarts *n.:* persons who firmly support a cause, especially of a political party

gadfly *n.:* a person who annoys others by rousing them from indifference

*indomitability *n.:* the quality of not being easily defeated or subdued

Marx and Engels: Karl Marx (1818–1883), German philosopher and economist who founded modern socialism; Friedrich Engels (1820–1895), German socialist leader and writer who was a colleague of Karl Marx

Lenin: Vladimir I. Lenin (1870–1924), Russian leader of the 1917 Communist revolution and premier of the Soviet Union from 1917 to 1924

Glossary and Vocabulary(cont.)

Stalin: Joseph Stalin (1879–1953), dictator and general secretary of the Soviet Union's Communist Party from 1929 to 1953

Mao Tse-tung: (1893–1976) revolutionary leader and chairman of the People's Republic of China from 1949 to 1959 and of the Chinese Communist Party from 1949 to 1976

dialectical and historical materialism: Dialectical materialism is the Marxist theory, adopted as the official philosophy of the Soviet Union, that maintains the objective reality of matter and its priority in importance over mind. Historical materialism is the part of dialectical materialism that holds that social ideas and institutions develop as the result of economic factors.

Chapter 9

sine qua non: Latin, literally *without which not,* an essential qualification; an absolute condition

*behest *n.:* a request or order

Chapter 11

seismic *adj.:* literally, having to do with earthquakes; here, used to connote radical change

*gregarious *adj.:* sociable

Chapter 12

Fugencio Batista: president of Cuba from 1940 to 1944, and again from 1952 to 1959 when he was ousted by Fidel Castro

*inauspicious *adj.:* unfavorable; not boding well

Chapter 13

*mandate *n.:* an authoritative

order; the wishes of a group conveyed to a representative or representatives of the group and regarded as an order

Che Guevara: (1928–1967) Cuban revolutionary leader under Fidel Castro who became a heroic figure to some, based on his idealism

Fidel Castro: (1926–) Cuban revolutionary leader; Cuban prime minister from 1959 to the present

Mussolini: Benito Mussolini (1883–1945), Italian Fascist dictator executed by his own people

Chapter 14

*traverse *v.:* to cross

*palatable *adj.:* acceptable to the mind or taste

parried *v.:* deflected, especially by giving an evasive response, as to a question or criticism

*ruminate *v.:* to turn something over in one's mind

solidarity *n.:* unity of purpose or interest

Chapter 15

*strictures *n.:* restricting conditions

*conducive *adj.:* that leads or contributes to an effect

*gambit *n.:* a maneuver or action intended to gain an advantage

Section II: Chapters 16–38
Chapter 16

*pinnacle *n.:* the highest point

Chapter 17

*impudent *adj.:* boldly disrespectful

polemics *n.:* arguments; controversial discussions

dyspeptic *adj.:* grouchy

Chapter 19

*eminently *adv.:* in a remarkable or noteworthy manner

*intimation *n.:* hint; suggestion

Chapter 20

*onus *n.:* burden of proof

sub judice: under consideration by a court

orotund *adj.:* pompous and bombastic, especially in speech and writing

in camera: in a judge's private office rather than in open court

*adjunct *n.:* something added, especially something that is secondary or not essential to the thing to which it is added

Chapter 21

*contingency *n.:* the condition of being dependent on chance or uncertain conditions

*esoteric *adj.:* beyond the understanding of most people

fortnight *n.:* a period of two weeks

reactionary *adj.:* of a movement back to a former condition, as in politics or economics; extreme conservatism

*machinations *n.:* secret plots, especially those with evil intent

ad hominem: attacking the character of a person rather than debating on logical grounds

*patently *adv.:* clearly; in an obvious manner

Chapter 22

in absentia: not present

appellate court: a court that has the jurisdiction to review appeals

Chapter 23

***ameliorate** v.:* to make better; to improve

***altruistic** adj.:* selfless; concerned for the well-being of others

Chapter 24

***nascent** adj.:* beginning to form or grow

Chapter 25

microcosm: *n.:* a community regarded as a miniature version of the larger world

Chapter 26

***stipulated** v.:* specified as a condition, as in an agreement

Chapter 27

***auspices** n.:* sponsorship

august *adj.:* awe-inspiring; worthy of respect

carte blanche: freedom to do as one pleases

Chapter 28

***dispensation** n.:* a release or exemption, as from an obligation or duty

Chapter 29

lime *n.:* a white substance used in making mortar and cement

***rudimentary** adj.:* basic; elementary

Chapter 30

***perfunctory** adj.:* done purely

as a matter of routine; done superficially

progressive *adj.:* favoring improvement through social or political reform

***vagaries** n.:* odd or unexpected actions

***impunity** n.:* freedom from punishment or penalty

Chapter 31

***quixotic** adj.:* foolishly impractical or idealistic

***elicit** v.:* to draw forth

Chapter 32

***bellicosity** n.:* eagerness to fight or quarrel

laissez-faire: the policy or practice of allowing people to act without interference

***acrimonious** adj.:* bitter and sharp in manner or speech

bourgeois: middle-class

***salutary** adj.:* promoting health; beneficial

***inculcated** v.:* impressed upon the mind by frequent repetition

Chapter 33

martinet *n.:* a stickler for rigid regulations

malingering *n.:* pretending to be ill in order to escape work; shirking

***tenure** n.:* the length of time during which one holds an office or position

Chapter 34

heresy *n.:* any opinion opposed to official views

Chapter 35

***conundrum** n.:* a riddle or puz-

zling question

cordon *n.:* a line or circle of police or soldiers

Chapter 36

***rescinded** v.:* revoked or canceled

***inimical** adj.:* hostile; adverse or like an enemy to

crucible *n.:* a severe test

mettle *n.:* courage; quality of spirit or character

thespian *n.:* an actor or actress

Chapter 37

niggling *adj.:* petty; fussy

***rectify** v.:* to correct; to set right

***parley** n.:* a talk or conference to settle a dispute

troika *n.:* a group of three

***acquiesced** v.:* consented quietly, without enthusiasm

***chastened** adj.:* subdued, as from a punishment intended to make one better

Section III: Chapters 39–74
Chapter 39

***regaled** v.:* entertained, as with something pleasing or amusing

Chapter 40

tableau *n.:* a dramatic scene

Chapter 41

***genesis** n.:* beginning; origin

***elucidated** v.:* made clear; explained

***indigent** adj.:* in poverty; needy

gratis *adv.:* without charge

Chapter 42

*animosity *n.:* a feeling of strong dislike or ill will

cause célèbre: a celebrated law case or controversy

Chapter 45

*audacious *adj.:* fearless; bold

*progeny *n.:* offspring

*hierarchy *n.:* a group of people or things arranged in order of rank

Chapter 46

*sedentary *adj.:* not active; characterized by much sitting about

*ephemeral *adj.:* transitory; short-lived

*visceral *adj.:* instinctive or emotional rather than intellectual; gut-level

Chapter 47

*trepidation *n.:* fearful anxiety or uncertainty

interdict *n.:* an official prohibition

Chapter 48

*expurgated *adj.:* edited or censored, as of objectionable material

Chapter 49

*solicitous *adj.:* showing concern or care for

*caveat *n.:* a warning or explanation to prevent misinterpretation; a formal notice directing one to refrain from some action

Chapter 50

*usurping *v.:* taking by force or without right

*coopt (co-opt) *v.:* to persuade an opponent to join one's own party or system

Chapter 51

*precipitate *adj.:* hasty or abrupt

locus *n.:* place

Chapter 52

tricameral *adj.:* made up of three legislative chambers, as some parliaments

Chapter 54

fait accompli: something already done that cannot be changed

Chapter 55

*mundane *adj.:* ordinary; common; everyday

Chapter 57

*disabuse *v.:* to rid of false ideas

*jettison *v.:* to discard something, especially something that is useless or burdensome

Chapter 58

*ensconced *v.:* settled comfortably

Chapter 61

*exacerbated *v.:* made more intense

*cipher *n.:* a nonentity; a person or thing of no importance

*pragmatist *n.:* one who is concerned with actual, everyday affairs rather than with theory

Chapter 62

*imbued *v.:* permeated or inspired

Chapter 63

*nonplused *adj.:* perplexed in such a way that one is unable to speak or act

*renege *v.:* to go back on a promise or agreement

Chapter 64

welter *n.:* a confusion or turmoil

boot *n.:* British, the trunk of an automobile

bonnet *n.:* British, the hood of an automobile

Chapter 67

*anathema *adj.:* detestable, abhorrent; also, *n.:* a detested thing or person

Chapter 68

indemnity *n.:* a legal exemption from a penalty incurred by one's actions

Chapter 69

aboriginal *adj.:* existing from the earliest times

Chapter 70

*moribund *adj.:* dying; having little vitality left

*fomenting *v.:* inciting; stirring up

Chapter 71

*untenable *adj.:* that cannot be defended

*vilified *v.:* defamed; slandered

Chapter 72

*bereft *adj.:* sadly deprived of, as by the death of a loved one

Chapter 74

*sacrosanct *adj.:* very holy

First Thoughts

1. In your opinion, what is the most admirable quality of Mandela's character? Explain.

Shaping Interpretations

2. Identify two aspects of Mandela's childhood that helped him **develop as a leader.** Explain how they did so.

3. Describe an event from Mandela's youth that causes him to think differently about human relationships, white oppression, or black identity.

4. Why does the ANC launch its "Defiance Campaign"? What is the significance of the campaign?

5. Within the ANC, what debate leads to the formation of Umkhonto we Sizwe, or MK? What is Mandela's position? Why?

6. **"Living underground . . . is not much of an adaptation for a black man in South Africa."** What does Mandela mean by this statement?

7. In the days preceding the trial, Mandela realizes that he himself has come to **symbolize** something for the people of South Africa. What does he symbolize? Why is Mandela's realization important?

Writing Opportunity

Write a script for a brief scene that dramatizes this event.

READING CHECK
a. What is the literal meaning of the African name, Rolihlahla?
b. Who becomes Mandela's guardian after the death of his father?
c. Why does Mandela leave Fort Hare without finishing his degree?
d. What is the literal meaning of the word *apartheid?*
e. Why does Mandela go underground?
f. Why does Mandela go on a tour of the African continent?
g. Who will represent Mandela in court?

Connecting with the Text

8. Mandela has mixed feelings about South Africa: He loves it because it is his homeland but hates what it has become under apartheid. Have you ever felt affection for a place, a person, or a group of people but also disliked things they did or became? Explain.

Extending the Text

9. Mandela writes that, as a young activist, he was "angry at the white man, not at racism." In your opinion, is it possible to be opposed to an abstract idea without being opposed to the people who advance that idea? Give examples from modern-day society to support your response.

Reading Strategies: Chapters 1–15

Long Walk to Freedom

Summarizing/Organizing Information

In the first part of his autobiography, Nelson Mandela describes important events from his youth and early adulthood. Organizing and summarizing these events will help you to see more clearly Mandela's growth as a leader.

Listed below are major events from Mandela's early life. Arrange these events in chronological order by writing each one next to a number. Then, inside each box, explain the significance of that event. Some answers have been given for you.

Tours African continent
Earns law degree
Educated in Wesleyan colleges

Arrested
Nationalists come to power
Father dies

Tried for treason
Forms ANC Youth League
Banned by government

1.	2.	3.
4. Forms ANC Youth League The Youth League broadens the appeal of the ANC. It is also Mandela's first experience directing a large-scale organization.	5.	6. Tried for treason
7.	8.	9. Arrested

FOLLOW-UP: Which event do you think was most crucial in Mandela's development? Write a paragraph explaining why.

Book Notes

Chapters 1–15, *Long Walk to Freedom*

The Lay of the Land: South Africa

Official Name: Republic of South Africa
Capitals: Cape Town (legislative), Pretoria (administrative), Bloemfontein (judicial)
Basic Unit of Money: rand (1 rand = 100 cents)
Languages: 11 languages, 3 primary (English, Zulu, and Afrikaans)

ZULU WOMAN

English	Zulu	Afrikaans
Hello	Sabona (sah-BOH-nah)	Hallo
Yes / No	Yebo (YEAH-baw) / Cha (TCHA)	Ja (YAH) / Nee (KNEE-uh)
Thank you	Ngiyabonga (ngee-yah-BONG-AH)	Dankie (DUNN-key)
What's your name?	Ubani Igama? (OO-BAH-neel GAH-ma)	Wat is jou naam? (vut iss yo NAHM?)
Goodbye	Sale Kahle (salla GAHSH-leh)	Totseins (TOT-seens)

FOR YOUR READER'S LOG

How do you trace your ancestry?

Quotation Corner

"A person is a person by virtue of other people."
—**Xhosa proverb**

History in a Nutshell:

Who Are the Xhosa?

Native people in South Africa are descended from different groups of people; the most numerous are the Zulu, found in the Kwazulu-Natal region; the Sotho, originating in the high grasslands area; and the Xhosa (pronounced KHO-zah), found along the Eastern Cape. Eighteen percent of South Africans are Xhosa.

The Xhosa are divided into chiefdoms, each with its own leader and dialect. The major chiefdoms are the Thembu, Bomvana, Mpondo, and Mpondomise. Chiefdoms are split into clans, each of which claims one common male ancestor. Nelson Mandela is a Xhosa tribe member from the Thembu chiefdom and the Madiba clan.

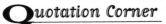

AFRICA

That Was Then: *A Xhosa Timeline*

- 1600s–1700s: Xhosa settle mountain regions
- 1700–1799: White colonists, Dutch missionaries arrive
- 1800: Ndlambe moves followers to Fish River
- 1811: Fourth of nine Frontier Wars ends, British push Xhosa east
- 1819: Nxele attacks Cape Town, is captured and imprisoned on Robben Island, escapes but drowns
- 1835: British assassinate Chief Hintsa
- 1852: Xhosa negotiate treaty to end Eighth Frontier War
- 1855: Epidemic kills Xhosa cattle; famine begins
- 1894: British conquer last Xhosa territory
- 1910: Union of South Africa formed (British and Dutch)
- 1948: Nationalist Party takes control, creates apartheid

Choices: Chapters 1–15

Building Your Portfolio

CREATIVE WRITING

Notes from the Underground

Write a series of three journal entries or letters that Nelson Mandela might have written while living underground. Include descriptions of his activities as well as his feelings.

ADVERTISING

Africa Awaits

Select one of the African countries Mandela visited during his 1962 tour of the continent. Research the country's past and present. What was it like when Mandela visited it? What is it like now? After gathering your information, create a travel brochure for potential visitors. Include a brief history of the country, descriptions and photos of its major cities and tourist attractions, and practical information such as languages spoken and foods commonly eaten. If possible, use a computer to publish your brochure.

ART AND COMMUNICATION

Prepare to Protest

With two or three other students, imagine that you are black South Africans participating in the ANC's National Day of Protest. (See book, pages 69–71.) First, think of a slogan—a catchy phrase or short verse—that tells what you are protesting. Then, create protest signs using poster board and paints or markers. Finally, prepare a brief, two- to three-sentence statement to give to the press in case you are asked to comment.

READING STRATEGIES

Building Background Information

Research one of the following laws passed by the Nationalist Party in the early 1950s:

- The Suppression of Communism Act
- The Population Registration Act
- The Group Areas Act
- The Separate Representation of Voters Act
- The Bantu Authorities Act

Prepare a short speech in which you describe the act and speculate on how it affected the everyday lives of blacks, Indians, or mixed-race South Africans.

Consider This . . .

I said it was wrong and immoral to subject our people to armed attacks by the state without offering them some kind of alternative . . . Would it not be better to guide this violence ourselves . . . by attacking symbols of oppression, and not people?

Restate Mandela's opinion in your own words. Toward what or whom does he believe violence, in this case, should or should not be directed?

Writing Follow-up: Persuasion ■

Do you agree with Mandela? In two to four paragraphs, defend or disagree with the idea that violence should sometimes be used to overcome oppression. Support your position with evidence from the text or history.

Book Notes

Create an activity based on **Book Notes, Issue 1.** Here are three suggestions.

- Research large cities in South Africa.
- Research the use of nonviolent protest in the United States.
- Research other groups of people that organized into chiefdoms and clans.

First Thoughts

1. Which aspect of prison life strikes you as the most difficult to bear? Why?

Shaping Interpretations

2. Describe Mandela's dress as he enters court to defend himself after being charged with illegal exit from the country. According to Mandela, what does his dress **symbolize?**

3. Describe the defendants' strategy during the Rivonia trial. What do the defendants plead? Why?

4. According to Mandela, what is the prisoner's greatest challenge? Why?

5. Mandela and his comrades consider life in prison to be a "microcosm" of what? What purpose do you think this idea serves?

6. What is Mandela's attitude toward the warders? Why?

7. Give an example of Mandela's use of **humor.** Why do you think humor is important in Mandela's story?

READING CHECK

a. What is the supreme penalty for sabotage and conspiracy at the time of the Rivonia trial?

b. What sentence do Mandela and the other defendants receive?

c. What kind of manual labor do Mandela and his comrades perform for thirteen years on Robben Island?

d. Describe a form of communication devised by the prisoners.

e. What do the prisoners do to pass the time while working?

f. Name one of three devastating personal traumas Mandela suffers in 1968–69.

Writing Opportunity

Write a character description of Mandela from a warder's point of view.

Connecting with the Text

8. **"Men, I think, are not capable of doing nothing, of saying nothing, of not reacting to injustice, of not protesting against oppression, of not striving for the good society and the good life. . . ."** Describe a time in your life when this seemed true or untrue for you or someone you knew.

Challenging the Text

9. The judge at Rivonia says that he "is by no means convinced that the motives of the accused were as altruistic as they wish the court to believe . . . [A]mbition cannot be excluded as a motive." Do you think Mandela honestly portrays himself and his motives? Or do you agree with the judge that even the noblest motives are rarely pure? Support your opinion with specific evidence drawn from the book or from history.

Reading Strategies: Chapters 16–38

Long Walk to Freedom

Making Inferences

As you read, you make inferences about characters' personality traits based on their words and actions. For example, if a character says, "Just the idea of parachuting made me want to faint," you might infer that the character is afraid of heights.

Read each of the quotations on the left from Mandela's autobiography. In the rectangle on the right, write an inference about Mandela that could be drawn from the quotation.

> **1.** I never seriously considered the possibility that I would not emerge from prison one day. . . . I always knew that someday I would once again feel the grass under my feet and walk in the sunshine as a free man.

Inference:

> **2.** Despite blistered and bleeding hands [from working at the quarry], we were invigorated. I much preferred being outside in nature, being able to see grass and trees. . . . It felt good to use all of one's muscles, . . . and there was simple gratification in building up mounds of stone and lime.

Inference:

> **3.** When [the warder] was just a few feet from me, I said, as firmly as I could, "If you so much as lay a hand on me, I will take you to the highest court in the land. . . ." At such times, one must put up a bold front despite what one feels inside.

Inference:

FOLLOW-UP: Choose a quotation above that might lead to more than one inference. Explain what the second inference might be, and then identify the words or phrases that open the quotation to different interpretations.

Book Notes

Chapters 16–38, *Long Walk to Freedom*

Personal Profile: Karl Marx (1818–1883)

Karl Marx, a German philosopher, developed a political theory that changed the world when he co-wrote *Communist Manifesto*. Marx believed that having things (food, clothes, luxuries) gives people power and that studying a country's economics reveals who is in control. He felt that when workers revolted and employers no longer oppressed them, a new and classless society would be born. Black South Africans, in a country where a small group of wealthy whites controlled the country, could identify with this thesis.

Karl Marx

> **History in a Nutshell:** *Robben Island*
>
> Robben Island is
> • Named for the Dutch word for "seals"
>
> • Small (five square miles), located off the coast of Cape Town
> • Formerly a leper colony (from 1846 to 1931)
> • A former maximum security prison

What They Were Reading: *Antigone*

Sophocles' famous play is a tragedy about a burial. Creon, the new king of Thebes, decrees that Polynices, the vanquished king, cannot be buried. Polynices's sister Antigone buries her brother anyway, arguing that heaven's law overrules mortal law. Creon uncovers the body and orders Antigone's death, but then fears that the gods will punish him. He reburies Polynices and tries to free Antigone, but she has hanged herself. When he hears of Antigone's death, Creon's son kills himself. His mother, Eurydice, then commits suicide, leaving Creon alone—to be punished by his grief.

Antigone buries Polynices

The Law of the Land: Separate AND Unequal

Starting in 1911, the government of South Africa enacted racial discrimination laws. By 1950, "apartheid," or apartness, covered all aspects of daily life. Residents were classified as *white, coloured* (mixed race), or *native;* later, *Asian,* which included Indians, was added. People could live only in areas designated for their race. Mixed marriages were forbidden. Native and coloured people could not vote, attend schools with whites, or hold certain jobs. Public amenities, such as parks, were separate and unequal.

Choices: Chapters 16–38

Long Walk to Freedom

Building Your Portfolio

Notes from the Underground

Imagine that you are one of the following:
- an American journalist reporting for your local newspaper
- a member of the Red Cross who writes for the organization's newsletter

You have recently visited Robben Island to gather information for an article you plan to write. While there, you toured the prison, interviewed the prisoners in Section B, and spoke privately with Nelson Mandela. Now it is time to write. Before you begin, think about your audience and the purpose or impact you want your article to have. When you have finished writing, exchange articles with someone who wrote from the other point of view. Read each other's articles and then discuss differences in purpose, tone, and content.

ART

Reconstruct Robben Island

Re-read the description of the Robben Island prison found on pages 196–197. Then, using wood, plaster, cardboard, aluminum foil, or other building materials, make a scale model of one of the following:
- the prison building
- Section B
- Mandela's cell

When you are finished, check a partner's model for accuracy based on the descriptions in the book. Display your model for the class.

DRAMATIC INTERPRETATION

How Do You Plead?

With a group of classmates, choose a portion of the Rivonia trial to dramatize. First, work together to translate the text into script form. Be sure to include significant words, moments, and characters. Then,

assign roles and discuss costumes and props. Finally, rehearse your drama. If other groups are dramatizing segments of the trial that come before or after yours, you may want to perform your pieces in chronological order.

Consider This . . .

I was made, by the law, a criminal, not because of what I had done, but because of what I stood for, because of what I thought, because of my conscience. Can it be any wonder . . . that such conditions make a man an outlaw of society?
At what point does Mandela say these words? For what *does* he stand? What *has* his conscience led him to do? What have been the consequences?

Writing Follow-up: Cause and Effect, Compare and Contrast

Summarize the situation Mandela is in when he makes the statement above. Then, explain the following in as much detail as you can:
- According to Mandela, what "conditions" have caused him to be an "outlaw"?
- Conversely, what causes would the government assign to Mandela's current situation?

Write two to four paragraphs. Be sure to support the claims you make with examples from the book.

Book Notes

Create an activity based on **Book Notes, Issue 2.** Here are three suggestions.

- Read Sophocles' play *Antigone* and write a review.
- Research Jim Crow laws in the United States and compare them to apartheid laws.
- Research another island prison in another country.

First Thoughts

1. If you could ask Mandela one question about his experience, what would it be?

Shaping Interpretations

2. What caused the uprising in Soweto? What resulted from the uprising?

3. How do the younger political prisoners on Robben Island view Mandela and the other older prisoners? How does Mandela respond to the younger men?

4. Mandela thinks of tending his garden as a **metaphor** for what? Explain.

5. **"Only free men can negotiate. Prisoners cannot enter into contracts. . . ."** When does Mandela say these words? What do they mean?

6. Where does Mandela cast his vote on April 27, 1994? What does this location **symbolize?**

7. Summarize what Mandela says at the conclusion of the book about the long walk to freedom.

READING CHECK

a. Why does Robben Island also come to be known as "the University"?

b. From where do Mandela and two other prisoners plan to make an escape?

c. How is the manuscript of Mandela's memoirs discovered?

d. Under what condition is Mandela offered his freedom in 1985?

e. What is the "Third Force"?

f. What award does Mandela receive in 1993?

Writing Opportunity

Write a poem or a paragraph that explores the symbolism of Mandela's garden.

Connecting with the Text

8. **I did not in the beginning choose to place my people above my family, but in attempting to serve my people, I found that I was prevented from fulfilling my obligations as a son, a brother, a father, and a husband. . . .** Describe a time when fulfilling one obligation kept you from fulfilling another. How did you feel? How might the situation itself have been avoided?

Extending the Text

9. Mandela dedicated his life to the cause of racial justice. In your opinion, what causes or issues in today's world are worthy of such a sacrifice? Explain.

Name _____ Date _____

Reading Strategies: Chapters 39–76

Long Walk to Freedom

Understanding Cause and Effect

Near the end of his autobiography, Mandela concludes that apartheid had not only negative effects on South Africans, but also unintended positive effects.

Read the following passage from *Long Walk to Freedom*. Then, use information from the passage and from Chapters 39–76 to express the effects in your own words and cite examples.

The policy of apartheid created a deep and lasting wound in my country and my people. All of us will spend many years, if not generations, recovering from that profound hurt. But the decades of oppression and brutality had another, unintended effect, and that was that it produced . . . men of such extraordinary courage, wisdom, and generosity that their like may never be known again. Perhaps it requires such depth of oppression to create such heights of character.

Cause:

APARTHEID

First Effect:

_____

_____

_____

_____

Examples from text:

_____

_____

_____

_____

_____

Unintended Second Effect:

_____

_____

_____

_____

Examples from text:

_____

_____

_____

_____

_____

FOLLOW-UP: Mandela himself created great change in South Africa. Write a paragraph that identifies an important action Mandela takes and two or three effects this action had.

Book Notes

Issue 3

Chapters 39–76, *Long Walk to Freedom*

south africa flag

Personal Profile:
Desmond Tutu (Born 1931)

In 1976, Desmond Tutu, a dean in the South African Anglican Church, sent a letter to newly elected Prime Minister Vorster, asking for an end to oppression: "I have a growing nightmarish fear that unless something drastic is done very soon then bloodshed and violence are going to happen in South Africa almost inevitably." Mere months after Tutu's letter, police in Soweto fired on children protesting laws ordering instruction in black schools to be in Afrikaans, not English.

Tutu became more outspoken in his criticisms after becoming general secretary of the South African Council of Churches; he addressed Pope John Paul II, and encouraged foreign countries protesting apartheid to impose economic sanctions against South Africa. In 1984, Desmond Tutu was awarded the Nobel Peace Prize and elected bishop of Johannesburg. As mob clashes escalated, some blacks began to resent Tutu's criticism of any form of violence. But Tutu continued to promote peaceful protest and, in 1986, he became archbishop, the highest member of South Africa's Anglican Church. Archbishop Tutu became a leader in the eyes of the world—though in his own country he could not hold office or even vote.

FOR YOUR READER'S LOG

What would you do on your first day of freedom in thirty years?

Quotation Corner

I think mainly the one (who inspires my music) . . . is Desmond Tutu. And Mr. Nelson Mandela. Both those people are extremely powerful because . . . they don't have a dark agenda to become rich and famous and all that kind of stuff. I guess the best way to say it is that anyone who has the highest goals in mind for people on the planet is my hero.*

—Carlos Santana, Grammy-winning guitarist

That Was the Year: 1989

- First free vote held in Soviet Union
- Last Vietnamese troops leave Cambodia
- Presidents Bush and Gorbachev end the Cold War
- Berlin Wall destroyed
- Chinese soldiers fire on student demonstrators in Tiananmen Square

The Law of the Land: VOTE!

After native Africans received the right to vote, 91 percent of the registered voters, some nineteen million South Africans, participated in national elections in 1994.

History in a Nutshell: *A Nation's Anthem*

South Africa had two national songs:

Nkosi Sikelel' iAfrika and *Die Stem*. When apartheid was abolished, they were combined, creating a new national anthem in Xhosa, Afrikaans, and English.

VOTE

Choices: Chapters 39–76

Building Your Portfolio

CREATIVE WRITING

Prison Poem

Choose a moment, event, setting, or object from Mandela's years in prison that you find particularly moving. Some topics you might consider include Mandela's writing and/or burying the manuscript of his autobiography; the beach where the prisoners worked; Mandela's first contact visits with his wife and daughter; or Mandela's release. Make a list of sensory details that help you imagine the scene. Then, make a list of emotions that the scene evokes or that one of the people in the scene may have felt. Finally, use your lists to write a poem about your topic. You might imagine that you are Mandela, one of his colleagues or family members, or a prison employee and write your poem from that point of view.

ART

Leave Your Stamp on South Africa

You have been asked by the current South African government to design a commemorative stamp featuring Nelson Mandela. Before you begin, research stamp design and study some recent examples of stamp portraiture. You may also want to familiarize yourself with other features of South African stamps such as values, symbols, and common colors. After you design your stamp, give a brief presentation in which you unveil your design and explain your research findings and your creative process.

DRAMATIC READING

Born Free

Prepare a dramatic reading of the last six paragraphs of the book. If possible, use lighting, music, or visual aids to enhance your reading. You might want to create a slide show to accompany your reading using downloaded images from the Internet.

Consider this . . .

I never sought to undermine Mr. de Klerk, for the practical reason that the weaker he was, the weaker the negotiations process. To make peace with an enemy one must work with that enemy, and that enemy becomes one's partner.
Paraphrase this quote. Does Mandela approach problems practically, idealistically, or both? Give examples.

Writing Follow-up: Problem-Solution ___

Summarize Mandela's problem and the solution he chooses. Provide specific examples from the book to support your summary. Then, explain and give an example of the kind of solution Mandela rejects. Do you agree with his reasoning? Why? If possible, give examples from your own experience. Write two to four paragraphs.

Book Notes

Create an activity based on **Book Notes, Issue 3.** Here are three suggestions.

- Research the words and music for the South African national anthem.
- Create a collage of the events in 1989.
- Research Bishop Tutu's Nobel Peace Prize speech.

Book Review

MAJOR CHARACTERS

Use the chart below to keep track of the characters in this book. Each time you come across a new character, write the character's name and the number of the page on which the character first appears. Then, jot down a brief description. Add information about the characters as you read. Put a star next to the name of each main character.

NAME OF CHARACTER	DESCRIPTION

FOLLOW-UP: A *dynamic character* changes in some important way as a result of the story's action. In a paragraph, trace the transformation of one dynamic character from the time the character is introduced through the conclusion of the novel.

Book Review *(cont.)*

Long Walk to Freedom

SETTING

Time ....

Most important place(s) ....

....

One effect of setting on plot, theme, or character ....

....

....

PLOT

List key events from the novel.

- ....   - ....
- ....   - ....
- ....   - ....

Use your list to identify the plot elements below. Add other events as necessary.

Major conflict / problem ....

....

Turning point / climax ....

....

Resolution / denouement ....

....

MAJOR THEMES

- ....
- ....
- ....

Literary Elements Worksheet 1

Long Walk to Freedom

Foreshadowing

Mandela frequently uses foreshadowing to make his already well-known story more suspenseful and to hold the reader's attention.

Below are some quotations that foreshadow later events. Summarize the event that each quotation foreshadows.

Quotation that foreshadows:	Summary of foreshadowed event:
I would not be so lucky in the future in my fight against the authorities at the [University College of Fort Hare].	
I did not relish being deprived of the company of my children. I missed them a great deal during those days, long before I had any inkling that I would spend decades apart from them.	
He urged me to send someone else. It was simply too risky, ... especially as I was newly returned and ready to push ahead with MK. This wise advice was overruled by everyone, including myself.	
I did not want our relationship to go the way of that [tomato] plant, and yet I felt that I had been unable to nourish many of the most important relationships in my life. Sometimes there is nothing that one can do to save something that must die.	

FOLLOW-UP: Why do you think foreshadowing is important in the autobiography of a well-known person?

Name _____ Date _____

Literary Elements Worksheet 2

Long Walk to Freedom

Anecdotes

In his autobiography, Mandela often tells amusing or touching stories. These brief stories, or anecdotes, allow the reader to share the intense emotions Mandela felt during his struggle. They also give the reader a glimpse of Mandela's human side.

In each empty "Anecdote" box, briefly summarize an anecdote that evokes the given emotion. In each empty "Emotion" box, list an emotion the anecdote evokes. Complete the last row on your own.

ANECDOTE	EMOTION
Mandela's college friend Paul Mahabane refuses to do a chore for a white magistrate. Pages 53–54	discomfort
  Pages _____	grief
While in disguise, Mandela attempts to attend a meeting, but the door is slammed in his face. Page 92	
  Pages _____	anger
Mandela is visited by his daughter Zeni and his newborn granddaughter. Pages 324–326	
  Pages _____	

FOLLOW-UP: Choose one of the anecdotes in the chart above. In a paragraph, explain what this anecdote reveals to you about Mandela.

Literary Elements Worksheet 3

Long Walk to Freedom

Symbol

A symbol is a person, place, thing, or event that stands both for itself and for something more than itself. In his writing, Mandela sometimes uses symbols to convey abstract ideas. He also discusses symbols that were important in the struggle to end apartheid.

In each small oval is a symbol Mandela uses or discusses in his autobiography. In the outer oval, state one or two possible meanings for the symbol. Complete the last set of ovals with a symbol of your own choice.

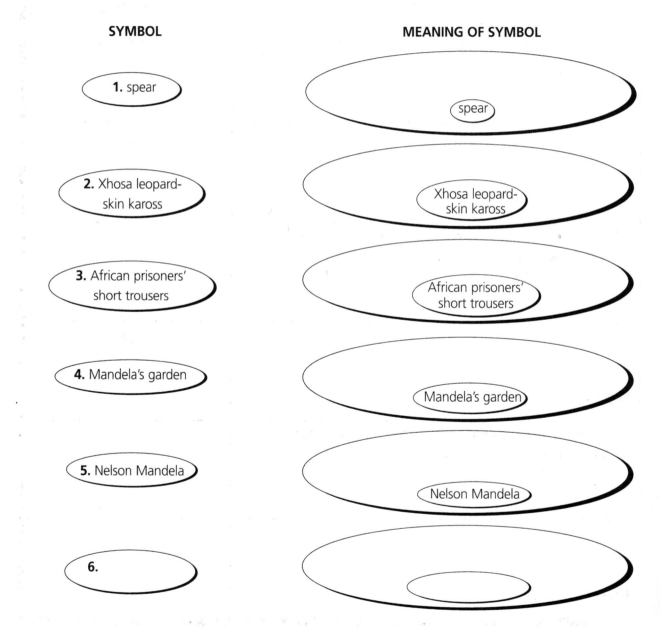

SYMBOL   MEANING OF SYMBOL

1. spear — spear

2. Xhosa leopard-skin kaross — Xhosa leopard-skin kaross

3. African prisoners' short trousers — African prisoners' short trousers

4. Mandela's garden — Mandela's garden

5. Nelson Mandela — Nelson Mandela

6.

FOLLOW-UP: Choose one of the symbols above. In a paragraph, explain how you think this symbol is connected to one of the book's major themes.

Literary Elements Worksheet 4

Long Walk to Freedom

Theme

A theme is the insight about life that is revealed in a literary work. It is usually developed throughout the course of the work. Authors develop their themes by including details of insights or events that relate to the theme.

• **Choose one of the themes listed in the box below, or think of another theme that is developed in** *Long Walk to Freedom.*
• **Write the theme in the center oval.**
• **In the outer boxes, give examples of insights or events that Mandela includes in the book to help develop this theme. Give at least one example from each of the book's three parts.**

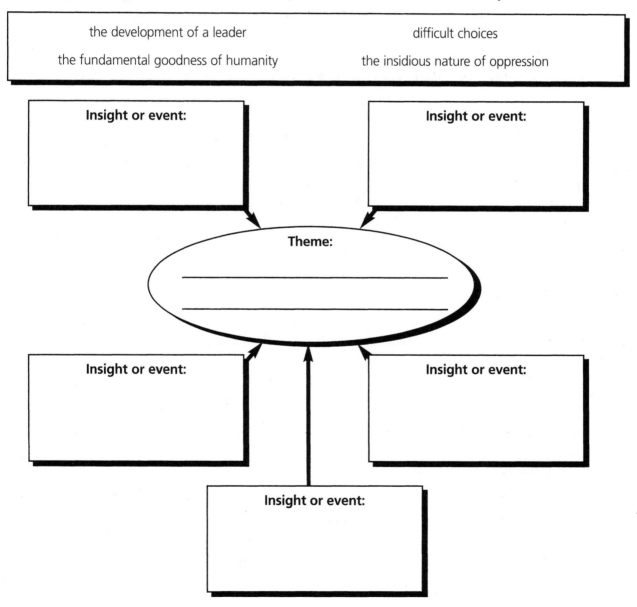

the development of a leader   difficult choices

the fundamental goodness of humanity   the insidious nature of oppression

Insight or event:

Insight or event:

Theme:

_____

_____

Insight or event:

Insight or event:

Insight or event:

FOLLOW-UP: Create a book cover for *Long Walk to Freedom* **that reflects or portrays the theme you explored above.**

Vocabulary Worksheet 1

Long Walk to Freedom

A. Circle the letter of the word or phrase that most nearly defines the italicized word in each excerpt from *Long Walk to Freedom*.

1. Although the role of chief was a *venerable* . . . one, it had, even seventy-five years ago, become debased by the control of an unsympathetic white government.
- **a.** improper
- **b.** respected
- **c.** honest
- **d.** traditional

2. Without being told, I soon *assimilated* the elaborate rules that governed the relations between men and women.
- **a.** absorbed
- **b.** rejected
- **c.** agreed to
- **d.** preferred

3. I trained in a *desultory* way, and only years later, when I had put on a few more pounds, did I begin to box in earnest.
- **a.** basic
- **b.** random
- **c.** strenuous
- **d.** unhurried

4. My plan . . . was simply to effect essentially cosmetic changes in order to make the ANC more intelligible—and *palatable*—to our allies.
- **a.** obvious
- **b.** significant
- **c.** official
- **d.** agreeable

5. I suggested that such a *gambit* be postponed until I was a convicted prisoner and the authorities were less cautious.
- **a.** public denial
- **b.** calculated move
- **c.** membership drive
- **d.** publicity campaign

6. I grasped how others came to the matter at hand directly, and who made a set of arguments *succinctly* and cogently.
- **a.** briefly
- **b.** persuasively
- **c.** dully
- **d.** emotionally

7. Unanimity, however, might be an agreement to disagree, to wait for a more *propitious* time to propose a solution.
- **a.** convenient
- **b.** favorable
- **c.** controversial
- **d.** open-minded

8. In short order, Malan began to implement his *pernicious* program.
- **a.** destructive
- **b.** hypocritical
- **c.** extensive
- **d.** ineffectual

Vocabulary Worksheet 1 (cont.)

9.[H]e was a keen debater and did not accept the *platitudes* that so many of us automatically subscribed to.

    a. doctrines   **c.** clichés

    b. regulations   **d.** settlements

10. The meeting had an *inauspicious* beginning.

    a. intrepid   **c.** informal

    b. unfavorable   **d.** unsettling

B. Read carefully the definition of each word. Then, write a sentence of your own using that word. If possible, include in your sentences clues to the meanings of the defined words.

11. axiom: *n.:* a statement that is accepted as true

_____

_____

12. cogently: *adv.:* in a forceful and compelling way; persuasively

_____

_____

13. obsequiously: *adv.:* in a fawning manner; showing too great a desire to obey or please

_____

_____

14. deference: *n.:* courteous regard or respect

_____

_____

15. taciturn: *adj.:* uncommunicative; generally silent

_____

_____

16. volition: *n.:* the act of making a deliberate and conscious choice

_____

_____

Vocabulary Worksheet 1 *(cont.)*

17. remonstrated: *v.:* said in protest or objection

_____

_____

18. gregarious: *adj.:* sociable

_____

_____

19. strictures: *n.:* restricting conditions

_____

_____

20. conducive: *adj.:* that leads or contributes to an effect

_____

_____

C. Circle the letter of the pair of words that best expresses a relationship similar to that expressed in the original pair.

21. emulation : admiration ::
   a. accusation : guilt
   b. appreciation : aversion
   c. apprehension : dread

22. missionary : proselytizing ::
   a. detective : reporting
   b. professor : educating
   c. actor : rehearsing

23. capitulate : conqueror ::
   a. operate : surgeon
   b. abdicate : successor
   c. legislate : politician

24. arbiter : decisive ::
   a. celebrity : famous
   b. author : reclusive
   c. candidate : defeated

25. ruminate : ignore ::
   a. criticize : condemn
   b. organize : rearrange
   c. exalt : degrade

Name _____ Date _____

Vocabulary Worksheet 2

Long Walk to Freedom

A. Circle the letter of the word or phrase that most nearly defines the italicized word in each excerpt from *Long Walk to Freedom*.

1. My request was ultimately granted, accompanied by a stern warning . . . that serious consequences would result if I returned to my *impudent* ways.
- **a.** unwarranted
- **b.** uninteresting
- **c.** sensible
- **d.** disrespectful

2. This was my first *intimation* that something had gone seriously wrong.
- **a.** decision
- **b.** hint
- **c.** evidence
- **d.** premonition

3. I had long argued that Communist literature was, for the most part, dull, *esoteric,* and Western-centered . . . .
- **a.** understood by few
- **b.** lacking relevance
- **c.** confined to economics
- **d.** condescending toward others

4. I am by no means convinced that the motives of the accused were as *altruistic* as they wish the court to believe.
- **a.** authoritative
- **b.** concealed
- **c.** selfless
- **d.** genuine

5. Firstly, they were brought in under the *auspices* of the government. . . .
- **a.** influence
- **b.** justification
- **c.** objections
- **d.** sponsorship

6. After the C.O.'s speech, we were handed picks and shovels and given *rudimentary* instructions as to the mining of lime.
- **a.** basic
- **b.** detailed
- **c.** uncertain
- **d.** uncivil

7. Regulations required that the authorities provide some official procedure for acknowledging our complaints. They did so . . . in the most *perfunctory* manner.
- **a.** superficial
- **b.** overbearing
- **c.** efficient
- **d.** formal

8. As a form of protest, they did not have a high success rate and the rationale behind them always struck me as *quixotic.*
- **a.** intentionally harmless
- **b.** dangerously combative
- **c.** foolishly impractical
- **d.** pointlessly unpleasant

Vocabulary Worksheet 2 (cont.)

Long Walk to Freedom

9. Over time, the debate concerning the ANC and the party became progressively *acrimonious*.
- **a.** agreeable
- **b.** bitter
- **c.** trivial
- **d.** idealistic

10. An advancement might take years to win, and then be *rescinded* in a day.
- **a.** reinstated
- **b.** authorized
- **c.** limited
- **d.** revoked

B. Read carefully the definition of each word. Then, write a sentence of your own using that word. If possible, include in your sentences clues to the meanings of the defined words.

11. pinnacle: *n.:* the highest point

_____

_____

12. eminently: *adv.:* in a remarkable or noteworthy manner

_____

_____

13. onus: *n.:* the burden of proof

_____

_____

14. patently: *adv.:* clearly; in an obvious manner

_____

_____

15. vagaries: *n.:* odd or unexpected actions

_____

_____

16. impunity: *n.:* freedom from punishment or penalty

_____

_____

Vocabulary Worksheet 2 *(cont.)*

Long Walk to Freedom

17. elicit: *v.:* to draw forth

_____

_____

18. inculcated: *v.:* impressed upon the mind by frequent repetition

_____

_____

19. inimical: *adj.:* hostile; adverse or like an enemy to

_____

_____

20. acquiesced: *v.:* consented quietly, without enthusiasm

_____

_____

C. Circle the letter of the pair of words that best expresses a relationship similar to that expressed in the original pair.

21. adjunct : network ::
 a. appendix : volume
 b. rhyme : poem
 c. ingredient : recipe

22. invent : ameliorate ::
 a. write : revise
 b. infect : taint
 c. enlist : desert

23. nascent : emerging ::
 a. commencement : completing
 b. inaugural : concluding
 c. final : terminating

24. conundrum : perplexes ::
 a. contract : requires
 b. film : directs
 c. mystery : uncovers

25. bellicosity : pacifist ::
 a. generosity : benefactor
 b. audacity : daredevil
 c. animosity : advocate

Vocabulary Worksheet 3

Long Walk to Freedom

A. Circle the letter of the word or phrase that most nearly defines the italicized word in each excerpt from *Long Walk to Freedom*.

1. Walter, perhaps the greatest living historian of the ANC, began to tell them about the *genesis* of the organization. . . .

    a. ideology   **c.** origin

    b. record   **d.** concept

2. [I]deas and theories were *elucidated* through the leaders asking and answering questions.

    a. explained   **c.** debated

    b. fixed   **d.** considered

3. South African law does not guarantee a defendant the right to legal representation, and thousands upon thousands of *indigent* men and women went to prison every year for lack of such representation.

    a. innocent   **c.** uninformed

    b. political   **d.** poor

4. Bantu education had come back to haunt its creators, for these angry and *audacious* young people were its progeny.

    a. noisy   **c.** bold

    b. intelligent   **d.** radical

5. [H]e was not swayed by the ephemeral and superficial values of the court, and made his decisions on a *visceral* understanding of his men and his people.

    a. imagined   **c.** literal

    b. instinctive   **d.** limited

6. Winnie was regarded with wariness and *trepidation*.

    a. dismay   **c.** rudeness

    b. disloyalty   **d.** uncertainty

7. One must be prepared for *precipitate* movements in prison, but one does not ever get used to them.

    a. violent   **c.** hasty

    b. postponed   **d.** deliberate

8. It is precisely those *mundane* activities . . . that one misses most in prison.

    a. personal   **c.** exceptional

    b. ordinary   **d.** family

Vocabulary Worksheet 3 (cont.)

Long Walk to Freedom

9. Once I was *ensconced* at Constantiaberge, I again began to meet with Kobie Coetsee and the secret committee.
   - **a.** settled
   - **b.** imprisoned
   - **c.** released
   - **d.** introduced

10. De Klerk was again *nonplused.* But this time my objections caused a reaction.
    - **a.** bewildered
    - **b.** indifferent
    - **c.** inflexible
    - **d.** contemptuous

11. Terror rose to the top of the ANC *hierarchy* in the general section, and was soon teaching ANC policies to other prisoners.
    - **a.** power structure
    - **b.** educational system
    - **c.** social clique
    - **d.** political process

12. To us, Mr. de Klerk was a *cipher.*
    - **a.** enemy
    - **b.** ally
    - **c.** spy
    - **d.** nonentity

13. But I found that such a meeting was *anathema* to ANC leaders in Natal.
    - **a.** unknown
    - **b.** abhorrent
    - **c.** necessary
    - **d.** unplanned

14. Joe explained that the passages read by Mr. de Klerk had been taken out of context and that Vula was a *moribund* operation.
    - **a.** nonexistent
    - **b.** hostile
    - **c.** dying
    - **d.** separate

15. Inkatha was attempting to postpone the election, but neither Mr. de Klerk nor I would budge. That day was *sacrosanct.*
    - **a.** holy
    - **b.** foreordained
    - **c.** essential
    - **d.** undiminished

B. Read carefully the definition of each word. Then, write a sentence of your own using that word. If possible, include in your sentences clues to the meanings of the defined words.

16. **animosity:** *n.:* a feeling of strong dislike or ill will

_____

_____

Vocabulary Worksheet 3 *(cont.)*

17. ephemeral: *adj.:* transitory; short-lived

_____

_____

18. expurgated: *adj.:* edited or censored, as of objectionable material

_____

_____

19. solicitous: *adj.:* showing concern or care for

_____

_____

20. coopt: *v.:* to persuade an opponent to join one's own party or system

_____

_____

21. disabuse: *v.:* to rid of false ideas

_____

_____

22. exacerbated: *v.:* made more intense

_____

_____

23. fomenting: *v.:* inciting; stirring up

_____

_____

24. vilified: *v.:* defamed; slandered

_____

_____

25. bereft: *adj.:* sadly deprived of, as by the death of a loved one

_____

_____

Book Projects

Writing About the Book

PLAY SCRIPT

Lucky Lessons

Choose two scenes from Mandela's life, one that occurs during his youth and one that occurs during his adulthood. The first scene should show Mandela learning a lesson about leadership, and the second should show the adult Mandela using or applying what he learned. Rewrite the scenes as scripts. Then, with several classmates, produce and perform the scenes for an audience. After your performance, challenge audience members to identify the theme of your vignettes.
(Creative Writing)

POSTSCRIPT

Still Walking?

Mandela's autobiography ends with his election to office in 1994. What happened next? Research Mandela's presidency and/or his retirement from office. Choose several highlights and write a paragraph or two summarizing each. Then, prepare a display using your paragraphs and, if possible, photos or other images that illustrate them. Present your findings to an audience or use it, and other classmates' displays, to create an exhibit for the school community.
(Critical Writing)

COMPARE AND CONTRAST

More or Less

Locate several biographies written about Mandela. Skim the books or scan their tables of contents or indexes to learn what topics they focus on. Then, choose an aspect of Mandela's life (up to his election as president) that is more thoroughly covered in one of the biographies than it is in the autobiography. Write an essay in which you compare and contrast how, and to what extent, each book treats the topic.
(Critical Writing)

LETTER TO THE AUTHOR

Dear Mr. Mandela

Write a letter to Nelson Mandela in which you do some or all of the following:
- Comment on the autobiography. What did you enjoy most about it? What did you enjoy least?
- Pose a question that was raised in your mind by the autobiography but not answered.
- Explain to him how the book has affected you. Did it cause you to think differently about something? Did it teach you something about yourself?

If possible, mail the letter to Mr. Mandela. (Your teacher may be able to help you locate an address.)
(Creative Writing)

LITERARY ANALYSIS

Do the Clothes Make the Man?

In his autobiography, Mandela occasionally remarks that he himself had become a symbol in South African society. Compose an essay in which you explain what Mandela came to symbolize and how he responded to his status as a cultural icon. What benefits resulted from this status? What hardships? Conclude your essay by reflecting more broadly on the human tendency to make icons or symbols out of individuals.
(Critical Writing)

CRITICAL RESPONSE

What's in a Name?

Re-read the first paragraph of the book. Then, write an essay explaining why you think Mandela's African name, Rolihlahla, does or does not reflect his true character. Support your opinion with specific examples from the book.
(Critical Writing)

Cross-Curricular Connections

HISTORY

Fellow Walkers

Research three or four of Mandela's colleagues, associates, or family members. Report back to the class on the roles and accomplishments of these individuals, their relationships with Mandela, and whether their portrayal in *Long Walk to Freedom* seems accurate. People you might research include Oliver Tambo, Evelyn Mandela (nee Mase), Winnie Mandela (nee Madikizela), Ahmed Kathrada, Mac Maharaj, Helen Joseph, Raymond Mhlaba, Albert Luthuli, Walter Sisulu, Joe Slovo, Robert Sobukwe, and Desmond Tutu.

MUSIC

African Anthems

Locate recordings of South Africa's two national anthems, *Die Stem,* the anthem of the old republic, and *Nkosi Sikelel' iAfrika,* the anthem of black South Africans. Research the origin and meaning of each song. Then, without revealing any background information, play the two anthems for a group of listeners. Challenge them to determine which anthem is which. Then, ask them what feelings or attitudes each anthem conveys. After the discussion, reveal the identities of the songs, translate the lyrics, and give a short presentation about their history.

GEOGRAPHY

Map It Out

Using materials of your choice, create two maps of the African continent. One should reflect the borders and names of countries as they existed in 1962, when Mandela toured the continent. On this map, chart Mandela's journey. Note what Mandela did at each of his stops, and use a color code and key to show which countries had waged successful campaigns for independence against their European colonizers. The second map should show Africa as it exists today. On this map note and explain any changes in country names or borders. Present your two maps to an audience of classmates.

JOURNALISM

Reporting from Rivonia

Research the coverage of either the Rivonia trial or Mandela's release from prison by the South African English-language media. Read newspaper and magazine articles and transcripts of radio reports, and, if possible, watch footage of television broadcasts. Then, imagine that you are a South African journalist living and working at that time. Create a series of three news stories—newspaper articles, radio reports, or television reports—covering the progress and conclusion of the trial. Your stories should reflect, as accurately as possible, the style and content of the reports you have studied, and they should feature quotations and/or commentaries from people involved in the trial. Read or present your stories to an audience.

LAW AND DRAMA

Apartheid in Action

With a small group of classmates, research the apartheid laws passed by South Africa's Nationalist government in the late 1940s and the 1950s. Read accounts of how these laws affected the everyday lives of black South Africans. Then, based on your findings, dramatize an aspect of life under apartheid. You might want to write and produce a short play about apartheid; or you might want to do dramatic readings of the laws (or other texts about apartheid) accompanied by music, mime, or expressive dance. Your purpose is to convey information about the laws while also showing the emotional or practical impact they had on black South Africans.

Multimedia and Internet Connections

NOTE: Check with your teacher about school policies on accessing Internet sites.

REPORT: FILM REVIEW

Same South Africa, Different Story

View videotapes of these two films: *Mandela and de Klerk* (Evergreen Entertainment, 1997), a docudrama about the negotiations between the two South African leaders; and *Cry, the Beloved Country* (1951), a fictional drama about race relations under apartheid. (If these films are not available, choose two other films about apartheid.) Then, write an essay comparing the two films, or work with a partner to review the films. How are their representations of apartheid the same? How are they different? Which gets the thumbs-up? Which doesn't? In your essay or discussion, identify different kinds of audiences that might appreciate each film.

AUDIO-VISUAL

You Show, He Tells

Locate recordings of some of Mandela's most famous speeches. Listen to them and choose one that you find particularly moving or effective. Then, arrange an audiovisual presentation of the recording for an audience. Using images downloaded from the Internet or photocopied from books or magazines, create a video or slide show to accompany the recorded speech. You might also want to include background music in your presentation. Your purpose is to use visual effects to enhance Mandela's delivery and message. After your presentation, invite audience members to comment.

TALK SHOW

Introducing Mr. Mandela

Work with a group of classmates to research Mandela's presidency and his private life since leaving office. Then, use the information to write and produce a television or radio talk show that features an interviewer, Mr. Mandela, and a studio audience that participates in a question-and-answer session after the interview. (You could script the Q-and-A session or pass out information cards to audience members and then allow them—and Mr. Mandela—to improvise.) Play the completed video or audiotape to an audience. Have them evaluate your production.

TELEVISION AD

Mandela Is Your Man!

It is 1994 and you are a member of the African National Congress campaign staff. Using computer-generated art or images downloaded from the Internet, create a television advertisement that persuades viewers to cast their votes for Mandela. After showing your ad to an audience, identify for them the persuasive devices you used. Then, hand out mock ballots on which your audience members can either vote for Mandela (if they find your ad persuasive) or offer advice for improvement.

COMPOSITION: MUSIC

Crescendo to Freedom

Map out the major phases of Mandela's life, from his lyrical boyhood in the veld to his triumphant achievements in later years. Choose three or four phases that you think are most important. Decide on the dominant mood or emotional tone of each phase. Then, compose a series of themes or short movements that, when played together, summarize Mandela's life. Play your music (or a recording of it) for an audience of listeners. After playing each movement, pause and challenge audience members to identify the phase of Mandela's life that is reflected in the music.

Introducing the Connections

The **Connections** that follow this novel in the HRW Library edition create the opportunity for students to relate the book's themes to other genres, times, and places and to their own lives. The following chart will facilitate your use of these additional works. Succeeding pages offer **Making Meanings** questions to stimulate student response.

Selection	Summary, Connection to Book
My People No Longer Sing Keorapetse Kgositsile *poem*	The defiance and optimism expressed in this poem evoke Mandela's indomitable spirit.
Something For The Time Being Nadine Gordimer *short story*	For most of his life, Mandela lived in a society where white people were given privileges over all others. This story explores the strain that the apartheid laws placed on the relationships of two couples, one white and one black. Although all four of the people in the stories believe that the laws are unjust, their differing methods of resistance isolate them from one another and reveal aspects of their characters that are previously unknown.
Oh, God, How Long Can We Go On? Desmond Tutu *book excerpt* **Biko** Peter Gabriel *song*	Although Mandela received horrendous treatment from the South African government, others were treated even worse. Tutu speaks out against the senseless murder of Steve Biko, a young political activist. Biko's death received international attention, and Peter Gabriel's song attests to this stunned awareness of an unnecessary death.
Sunlight in Trebizond Street Alan Paton *short story*	This story explores the psychological effects of imprisonment and interrogation. A political prisoner is tormented in very much the same way Mandela was, but the fates of the two men are far different.
Saint Crispian Day Speech from *Henry V* William Shakespeare *drama*	This speech—a rallying of the troops—is similar to Mandela's address at the Rivonia trial: passionate and fearless.

Introducing the Connections (cont.)

Selection	Summary, Connection to Book
Prologue Anna Akhmatova *poem*	This poem tells the sad tale of a Russian woman whose son is arrested and sentenced to death. Unlike Mandela and his family and friends, the woman is ultimately defeated by her grief and her inability to save her son.
South African Panel's Report Arrives in a Swirl of Bitterness Suzanne Daley *newspaper article*	It is always good to hear all sides of a story. South Africa's Truth and Reconciliation Commission investigated violations of human rights during apartheid, with controversial results. Almost every political group in South Africa is accused of crimes.
The Last White Man Graham Boynton *book excerpt*	The future of a liberated South Africa is examined in this selection by a white South African. Although far from optimistic, the author suggests that, under Mandela's leadership, South Africa has a chance to escape the economic and political deterioration that has followed the withdrawal of colonial rule throughout Africa.
Epilogue: Confronting the Ghosts Allister Sparks *book excerpt*	Hendrik Verwoerd was by far the most vicious proponent of apartheid in South Africa. Almost thirty years after his death, Verwoerd's grandson joined the ranks of one of his grandfather's most hated political opponents, the ANC. This selection explores how the younger Verwoerd renounced his grandfather's views and what his membership in the ANC signifies for the rest of South Africa.

Exploring the Connections

Making Meanings

Connecting with the Book

How do the lines "We emerge to prove Truth cannot be enslaved / In chains or imprisoned in an island inferno" reflect Mandela's actions while imprisoned?

1. Consider the last lines of the second stanza, "Retrieving songs almost aborted / On once battered black lips."* What is the significance of these lines?

2. How does the **tone** of the poem change between the third and fourth stanzas?

3. What is the effect of the **imagery** in the first stanza?

READING CHECK

a. According to the speaker, who "cannot remember"?*

b. Who does the speaker address in the fourth stanza?

Something for the Time Being

Connecting with the Book

Compare and contrast Daniel's situation with Mandela's as a young man.

1. Describe Ella and Daniel's relationship. How is it similar to Madge and William's? How is it different?

2. Do you think William should have allowed Daniel to wear his Congress button? Why or why not?

3. What does Madge mean when she says, "I'm not angry. I'm beginning to get to know you"?

READING CHECK

a. Why has Daniel lost his job with the Dalzin Brothers?

b. Who is Flora Donaldson?

c. Why does William Chadders tell Daniel that he cannot wear his Congress button?

Oh, God, How Long Can We Go On? and Biko

Connecting with the Book

How does the international reaction to Biko's death compare to the international reaction to the Rivonia trial and subsequent convictions?

1. What do you think the minister of police meant when he said that Biko's death "leaves me cold"?

2. Why did the death of one young man have such a significant impact on South Africa and the world?

3. In the Peter Gabriel song, what is the meaning of the lines, "You can blow out a candle / But you can't blow out a fire / Once the flames begin to catch / The wind will blow it higher"?**

READING CHECK

a. Why was Steven Biko killed?

b. What did the UN do as a result of Biko's death?

c. Why, according to Desmond Tutu, should all people be treated equally?

*From "My People No Longer Sing" from *7 South African Poets* by Keorapetse Kgositsile. Reprinted by permission of **Keorapetse Kgositsile**.

From lyrics to "Biko" by Peter Gabriel. Copyright © 1980 by Real World Music Ltd. All rights reserved. International Copyright Secured. Reprinted by permission of **Real World Music and Lipservices.

Making Meanings

Connecting with the Book

How does the speaker's attitude toward political struggle differ from Mandela's?

1. What type of organization is the People's League?

2. How does the speaker change from the beginning of the story to the end?

3. What do you think will happen to the speaker after the end of the story?

READING CHECK

a. How long has the speaker been imprisoned at the beginning of the story?

b. What information does Casper try to get out of the speaker?

c. How did the speaker break his promise to the People's League?

Saint Crispian Day Speech

Connecting with the Book

What does this speech have in common with Mandela's courtroom address at the Rivonia trial?

1. What do you think is the purpose of this speech?

2. How does the speaker feel about the battle?

READING CHECK

a. What event is taking place, or is about to take place, at the time of the speech?

b. According to the speaker, how will the men feel who do not fight on Crispian's day?

Prologue

Connecting with the Book

How are the speaker's actions different from those of Winnie Mandela while Nelson was imprisoned? Why do you think the two women behave so differently?

1. **Personification** means giving human qualities to an object or animal. List two instances of personification that occur in the poem.

2. What does the speaker mean when she says, "Son in irons and husband clay"?

READING CHECK

a. In what country does the speaker in the poem live?

b. What happens to the speaker at the end of the poem?

3. What type of relationship do you think the speaker has with her son? Use specific details from the poem to support your response.

Making Meanings

South African Panel's Report Arrives in a Swirl of Bitterness

1. What happened to the people who confessed everything to the commission? Do you think that these consequences are adequate?

2. If you consider the reception of the report, what is **ironic** about the name "Truth and Reconciliation Commission"?

3. Does it surprise you that a black party (Inkatha) aided the state in maintaining its power? Why or why not?

READING CHECK

a. Which political party supported the findings of the Truth and Reconciliation Committee?

b. According to the report, which group committed the greatest number of human rights violations?

c. List two of the violations that the ANC is accused of committing.

The Last White Man

1. **Tone** is the attitude the writer takes toward the subject of a work. What seems to be the tone of this selection?

2. The writer states that "My Victorian antecedents brought with them to Africa the benefits of . . . a new god." What does his statement suggest about the religions that were replaced by the "new god"?

3. At one point the writer says that the labor force in South Africa is "notoriously underproductive," and in the following paragraph he says that there is a "highly productive white community." Which group do these statements imply is "notoriously underproductive"?

READING CHECK

a. According to the selection, what happened to most of the colonized African countries after they gained independence?

b. How many of the world's twenty poorest countries are located in Africa?

c. What type of education system did the Afrikaners set up for blacks in South Africa?

Making Meanings

Connecting with the Book

How does Wilhelm Verwoerd's presence in the ANC reflect Mandela's mission to "liberate the oppressed and the oppressor both"?

1. Why do you think so many Afrikaners joined either the ANC or the parties of the far right after the end of apartheid?

2. How did Wilhelm's education help him to gain a new perspective on South African politics?

3. What does Wilhelm mean when he says, "It [the past] must all come out so that the sunlight can heal the wounds"?

READING CHECK

a. Who was Hendrik Verwoerd?

b. How was he related to Wilhelm Verwoerd?

Name _____ Date _____

TEST   PART I: OBJECTIVE QUESTIONS

In the space provided, mark each true statement *T* and each false statement *F*. (20 points)

_____ **1.** As a boy, Nelson Mandela resents white South Africans.

_____ **2.** Mandela is ashamed to wear his father's oversized clothes on his first day of school.

_____ **3.** Mandela earns his bachelor's degree at the University College of Fort Hare.

_____ **4.** As soon as the treason trial is concluded Mandela goes underground.

_____ **5.** Mandela has no regrets about the choice he made to commit his life to the struggle against apartheid.

_____ **6.** During his African tour, Mandela has to convince leaders of other African countries that the ANC is not a communist organization.

_____ **7.** It is easy for the Robben Island prisoners to communicate with one another during the first few years of their sentences.

_____ **8.** Mandela begins negotiations with the South African government only after discussing the matter with his comrades.

_____ **9.** Mandela believes that there is goodness within every human being.

_____ **10.** In 1993, F. W. de Klerk and Nelson Mandela are jointly awarded the Nobel Peace Prize.

Complete each statement by writing the letter of the best answer in the space provided. (10 points)

11. Mandela's given name, Rolihlahla, literally means _____.
    a. wanderer   **c.** loyal one
    b. son of the chief   **d.** troublemaker

12. At the end of the Rivonia trial, Mandela and the other defendants are sentenced to _____.
    a. death   **c.** thirty years in prison
    b. life in prison   **d.** manual labor

13. Mandela refuses to wear _____.
    a. a leopard-skin kaross   **c.** short trousers
    b. a three-piece suit   **d.** his father's pants

14. Robben Island is also known as _____.
    a. The University   **c.** The Gilded Cage
    b. The Dungeon   **d.** The Capital

15. Winnie Mandela was arrested and tried for _____.
    a. sabotage and treason   **c.** refusing to carry a pass
    b. breaking and entering   **d.** kidnapping and assault

TEST   PART II: SHORT-ANSWER QUESTIONS

Answer each question, using the lines provided. (40 points)

16. When Mandela is in school at Healdtown, he hears the Xhosa poet Krune Mqhayi speak. What effect does Mqhayi have on Mandela?

_____

_____

_____

17. Why does Mandela come to be known as "the Black Pimpernel"?

_____

_____

_____

18. Explain Mandela's position on the issue of an armed struggle.

_____

_____

_____

19. Give two reasons why Mandela tours the African continent.

_____

_____

_____

20. How does Mandela finally get arrested? With what is he charged?

_____

_____

_____

Name _____ Date _____

21. Why does Mandela decide to represent himself at his trial?

_____

_____

_____

22. Who does Mandela say is the "most important person in any prisoner's life"? Why?

_____

_____

_____

23. Why does Mandela call his living arrangements at Victor Verster prison "a gilded cage"?

_____

_____

_____

24. Summarize Mandela's attitude toward F. W. de Klerk.

_____

_____

_____

25. What is the outcome of the election held in South Africa in April 1994?

_____

_____

_____

TEST PART III: ESSAY QUESTIONS

Choose *two* of the following topics. Use your own paper to write two or three paragraphs about each topic you choose. *(30 points)*

a. Near the end of the book, Mandela comments that apartheid has "created a deep and lasting wound" in South Africa, but that this wound has produced many individuals of "courage, wisdom, and generosity." He then wonders whether "it requires such depth of oppression to create such heights of character." Does it, in your opinion? In your response, consider Mandela himself and at least one other respected historical figure.

b. Identify and explain two sacrifices Mandela makes in order to devote himself to the struggle. In your opinion, is the outcome worth the sacrifice? Why?

c. What do you consider to be Mandela's greatest strength as a leader? Support your opinion with specific examples from the book.

d. Discuss how clothing functions symbolically in Mandela's autobiography.

e. Discuss how one of the **Connections** from the back of the book (HRW LIBRARY edition) is related to a theme, issue, or character in *Long Walk to Freedom*.

Use this space to make notes.

Answer Key

Answer Key

Chapters 1–15

■ Making Meanings

> **READING CHECK**
>
> **a.** The name Rolihlahla means "troublemaker."
>
> **b.** The Thembu king becomes Mandela's guardian.
>
> **c.** He has been suspended for refusing to assume an office to which he has been elected, and he feels that he is being unfairly pressured to go against his principles.
>
> **d.** *Apartheid* literally means "apartness."
>
> **e.** He has been banned by the government.
>
> **f.** Mandela visits other African nations to solicit their support for the ANC and also to receive military training.
>
> **g.** Mandela will represent himself.

1. Responses will vary. Qualities students are likely to admire include Mandela's commitment to an ideal, his sense of self-discipline, his humility, his selflessness, his courage.

2. Responses will vary but may include one of the following: While playing and working with other boys in the veld, Mandela learned to fight fairly and never to dishonor his opponent; from his father, a Thembu chief, Mandela learned to rebel against injustice; as a steward in the household of the Thembu king, Mandela learned the basic principles of democracy.

3. Responses will vary but may include one of the following: When Mandela first sees the home of the Thembu king, he begins to realize that people can achieve different degrees of wealth and power; when he hears Chief Meliqqili speak after his circumcision he considers for the first time (but then rejects) the idea that the white man is an oppressor rather than a benefactor; when at Healdtown, Mandela meets a couple who have different tribal backgrounds, and he begins to realize that he is an African, not just a Thembu; when he hears the poet Mqhayi speak at Healdtown, his identification with other Africans becomes even stronger; when his friend Paul stands up to a local magistrate, he begins to realize that a black person can choose not to accept insults.

4. The ANC launches its Defiance Campaign in response to a series of apartheid laws passed by the new Nationalist government. The campaign is significant because it is the largest organized resistance movement yet; it gives the ANC a great deal of publicity; it causes the ANC's membership to increase dramatically.

5. The debate that leads to the formation of MK concerns whether the ANC should continue on its course of nonviolent protest or begin employing more militant forms of protest. Mandela believes that the ANC should use violent means of protest because a strategy (such as nonviolence) should be used only as long as it works and because the government is using more and more violence to suppress the resistance. (Accept either reason.)

6. Mandela means that black South Africans already live a kind of underground life: Their actions are constantly monitored; their motives are constantly questioned; it is difficult for them to trust anything or anyone; they must always play a role that is not in keeping with who they feel they are.

7. Mandela realizes that he symbolizes the movement itself—the struggle for justice in an unjust society. This realization is important because it helps him to see that, as a public symbol, he can advance his cause simply by being visible.

8. Responses are personal and need not be shared.

9. Some students will feel that it is possible—and morally preferable—to oppose ideas rather than people. Others will feel that ideas have no existence without the people who hold them, and that those who believe they are opposed only to an idea are being dishonest. Students' responses should be supported by one or more real-life examples.

■ Reading Strategies Worksheet

Summarizing/Organizing Information

Events are listed in chronological order. Explanations of events' significance may vary. Possible responses are provided.

1. **Father dies:** After his father's death, Mandela goes to live with the Thembu king, at whose court he learns the basic principles of democracy.

2. **Educated in Wesleyan colleges:** These schools helped "westernize" Mandela and his peers but also helped broaden Mandela's horizons.

3. **Earns law degree:** A law degree enables Mandela to open the first black law firm in Johannesburg and begin defending victimized Africans.

4. **Forms ANC Youth League:** The Youth League broadens the appeal of the ANC and stages mass demonstrations. It is also Mandela's first experience as director of a large-scale organization.

5. **Nationalists come to power:** The Nationalists impose the system of apartheid on South Africa.

6. **Tried for treason:** During this lengthy trial Mandela's marriage and law firm fail.

7. **Banned by government:** When he and the ANC are banned, Mandela decides to go underground.

8. **Tours African continent:** Mandela's first excursion outside South Africa; he learns about the ANC's international reputation and receives military training.

9. **Arrested:** From jail Mandela is less able to actively direct the movement, but he realizes his symbolic role.

FOLLOW-UP: Responses will vary. Students may cite the formative experience of growing up in the Thembu court.

Chapters 16–38

■ Making Meanings

READING CHECK

   a. The supreme penalty for these crimes is death.

   b. Their sentence is life imprisonment.

   c. They mine lime in a quarry.

   d. Accept any of the following: They placed written messages under false bottoms in discarded match-boxes; they placed messages wrapped in plastic in the bottom of food drums or under toilet seats; they wrote messages using milk, which became invisible as it dried; they wrote messages on toilet paper; they communicated with other prisoners in the prison hospital.

   e. They debate.

   f. His mother dies and he is not allowed to attend her funeral; Winnie is arrested, brutally interrogated, and imprisoned; his son Thembi dies in a car accident.

1. Responses will vary. Students may cite the physical hardships or the emotional strain.

2. Mandela enters the courtroom wearing a leopard-skin kaross, the traditional dress of the Xhosa warrior, rather than the suit and tie common in Western societies. Mandela chose this dress to emphasize how unfair it was for him, a black African, to be standing in the middle of a white man's court. The kaross also symbolized his contempt for the hypocritical manners of the white man's legal system.

3. The defendants use the trial as a way to advance their own beliefs. Rather than attempt to defend themselves, they decide to put the state itself on trial. They do not deny any of the accurate charges, but rather argue that the charges and the laws themselves are unjust. In keeping with the belief that the government is the guilty party, the defendants plead "not guilty."

Answer Key (cont.)

Long Walk to Freedom

4. Mandela believes that the prisoner's greatest challenge is to preserve and even build up one's inner strength. This is difficult to do because prison is designed to break the spirit and destroy individuality.

5. Mandela and his comrades consider the struggle for justice in prison to be a microcosm of the larger struggle for justice being waged outside the prison walls. This idea gives their suffering some meaning; it gives them a reason to persevere.

6. Mandela and his comrades all realize that warders are the most important people in their lives. They attempt to befriend the warders for two reasons: It is self-defeating to make enemies out of them; and they believe that all people are capable of changing for the better.

7. Examples of humor will vary but should come from the text. Students should draw one of the following conclusions about the importance of humor: Humor is one way the prisoners cope with their trying circumstances; Mandela uses humorous moments to contrast with more horrifying moments; Mandela uses humor to show that life in prison could sometimes be "normal."

8. Responses are personal and need not be shared.

9. Some students will feel that Mandela's motives are totally pure and that this rare selflessness makes him a great man. These responses should be supported with examples of Mandela's own altruism or that of other great figures in history. Other students will respond that all great leaders are at least partly motivated by ambition and that Mandela is no exception. These responses may be supported by examples of Mandela's self-regard (for example, as a "symbol of justice in the court of the oppressor" or his youthful dreams of greatness).

■ Reading Strategies Worksheet

Making Inferences

Inferences may vary. Possible responses are given.

1. Mandela is an optimist.

2. Mandela is a person who tries to make the best out of every situation.

3. Mandela has the ability to act courageously even when he is afraid.

FOLLOW-UP: Responses will vary. Students should provide alternative interpretations of the quotes and then point to words or phrases that create ambiguity.

Chapters 39–76

■ Making Meanings

> **READING CHECK**
>
> **a.** It is known as "the University" because Mandela and his comrades organize and teach formal courses to one another based on their areas of expertise.
>
> **b.** They plan to escape from a dentist's office in Cape Town.
>
> **c.** Mandela buries the manuscript in the courtyard and then it is dug up by workmen.
>
> **d.** Mandela is promised freedom if he unconditionally rejects political violence.
>
> **e.** The "Third Force" is the name Mandela gives to a group he infers exists—militants whose probable purpose is to disrupt negotiations.
>
> **f.** Mandela is awarded the Nobel Peace Prize.

1. Responses will vary. Students might focus on an aspect of prison life, family life, or advice for the future.

2. The uprising in Soweto began when 15,000 students gathered to protest the government's requirement that half of all high school classes must be taught in Afrikaans. The police responded to the protest with violence, and this, in turn, sparked riots and violence throughout the country.

3. The younger, more radical and aggressive prisoners consider Mandela and his comrades to be old-fashioned and hopelessly moderate. Mandela tries to listen to and understand the young men's point of view, but he feels that their behavior is immature and their philosophy shortsighted.

4. Mandela thinks of tending his garden as a metaphor for leadership. Like a gardener, a leader must plant seeds, harvest and take responsibility for the results, attempt to repel enemies, preserve what is valuable, and weed out what is not.

5. Mandela says these words in a speech (read by his daughter) in which he rejects the conditional offer of freedom extended to him by the government in 1985. He means that, as both a prisoner and a black South African, he does not have the freedom to strike bargains with those who are in power. Even if he accepts this offer, he says, neither he nor his people will lead a truly free life as long as apartheid is in effect.

6. Mandela casts his vote in Natal near the grave of the first president of the ANC. His action is symbolic because he hopes to show the people of Natal that it is safe to vote and to give them hope that the violence will end. It is also symbolic because it brings the struggle for freedom full circle.

7. Mandela says that the long walk to freedom is not yet over. South Africans, he says, must learn now to live in a way that respects the freedom of all people. Mandela acknowledges that with freedom comes great responsibility, and that living a responsible life will be the great challenge of the next phase of the journey.

8. Responses are personal and need not be shared.

9. Responses will vary. Students might mention the end of hunger, the reduction of pollution, or the fostering of understanding among races.

■ Reading Strategies Worksheet

Understanding Cause and Effect

Responses may vary. Possible responses are given.

First Effect: deep pain for South Africans

Example: Thousands of South Africans lost their lives in the armed struggle.

Unintended Second Effect: people of extraordinary character

Example: Mandela spent almost thirty years in prison.

FOLLOW-UP: Responses will vary.

Literary Elements Worksheets

■ Foreshadowing

1st quotation—foreshadows the conflict Mandela will later have with the principal of the college when he refuses to assume the office to which he has been elected. This conflict will lead to his withdrawal from the college.

2nd quotation—foreshadows Mandela's lengthy prison sentence.

3rd quotation—foreshadows Mandela's arrest after meeting with the ANC chief to tell him about his tour of the African continent.

4th quotation—foreshadows the end of Nelson and Winnie's marriage.

FOLLOW-UP: Many readers will be familiar with the major events of a well-known person's life, and so foreshadowing helps make the story suspenseful once again.

■ Anecdotes

Responses will vary. Sample responses are given.

ANECDOTE	EMOTION
Mandela's college friend Paul Mahabane refuses to do a chore for a white magistrate. Pages 53–54	discomfort
Mandela discovers that his son has died in a car wreck and is comforted by his friend Oliver Tambo. Pages 269–270	grief
While in disguise, Mandela attempts to attend a meeting, but the door is slammed in his face. Page 92	amusement
A prison official insults Mandela's wife, Winnie, and Mandela loses his temper. Pages 298–299	anger
Mandela is visited by his daughter Zeni and his newborn granddaughter. Pages 324–326	joy
Responses will vary.	Responses will vary.

FOLLOW-UP: Responses will vary.

■ Symbol

Possible meanings for each symbol may vary slightly. Sample meanings are given.

1. **Spear:** black South Africans' struggle against apartheid; a spirit of militarism

2. **Xhosa leopard-skin kaross:** Mandela's tribal roots; the injustice of a black man in a white man's court

3. **African prisoners' short trousers:** black Africans' status as "boys," or second-class citizens

4. **Mandela's garden:** a leader's effort to nurture, preserve, and tend to his followers or his cause

5. **Nelson Mandela:** rebellion; the struggle for justice

6. Responses will vary.

FOLLOW-UP: Paragraphs will vary.

■ Theme

Examples for each theme will vary. Sample responses are given.

the development of a leader: Mandela's exposure to democracy in the king's court as a boy (Part I); Mandela's willingness to die for his cause during the Rivonia trial (Part II); Mandela's diplomatic negotiations with the South African government (Part III)

difficult choices: Mandela's decision to leave Fort Hare rather than violate his principles (Part I); Mandela's decision to go underground (Part II); Mandela's decision to initiate negotiations without the knowledge and consent of his colleagues (Part III)

the fundamental goodness of humanity: Mandela's belief that one should preserve the dignity of one's enemy even while defeating him or her (Part I); Mandela's efforts to educate prison warders and officials and thereby tap into their goodness (Part II);

Mandela's belief that one's enemy must also be one's partner (Part III)

the insidious nature of oppression: Mandela's youthful regard for the European colonizers of South Africa as benefactors (Part I); Mandela's occasional slip into prejudicial thinking (Part II); the South African government's development of a Third Force to encourage conflict among black South Africans.

FOLLOW-UP: Book covers will vary but should reflect the theme students focused on in the graphic organizer.

Vocabulary Worksheets

If you wish to score these worksheets, assign the point values given in parentheses.

■ Vocabulary Worksheet 1

A. *(4 points each)*

1. b. respected	6. a. briefly
2. a. absorbed	7. b. favorable
3. b. random	8. a. destructive
4. d. agreeable	9. c. clichés
5. b. calculated move	10. b. unfavorable

B. *(4 points each)*

11.–20. Responses will vary.

C. *(4 points each)*

21. c. apprehension : dread
22. b. professor : educating
23. b. abdicate : successor
24. a. celebrity : famous
25. c. exalt : degrade

■ Vocabulary Worksheet 2

A. *(4 points each)*

1. d. disrespectful	6. a. basic
2. b. hint	7. a. superficial
3. a. understood by few	8. c. foolishly impractical
4. c. selfless	9. b. bitter
5. d. sponsorship	10. d.revoked

B. *(4 points each)*

11.–20. Responses will vary.

C. *(4 points each)*

21. a. appendix : volume
22. a. write : revise
23. c. final : terminating
24. a. contract : requires
25. c. animosity : advocate

■ Vocabulary Worksheet 3

A. *(4 points each)*

1. c. origin	9. a. settled
2. a. explained	10. a. bewildered
3. d. poor	11. a. power structure
4. c. bold	12. d. nonentity
5. b. instinctive	13. b. abhorrent
6. d. uncertainty	14. c. dying
7. c. hasty	15. a. holy
8. b. ordinary	

B. *(4 points each)*

16.–25. Responses will vary.

Exploring the Connections

■ My People No Longer Sing

> **READING CHECK**
> **a.** The speaker says that "the dead cannot remember."
> **b.** The speaker addresses Nelson Mandela.

1. Responses will vary. These lines imply the violence black South Africans have been subjected to in the struggle for freedom.

2. The tone of the poem changes from painful resignation to powerful defiance.

3. Responses will vary. Students may suggest that imagery suggests isolation and confusion.

Connecting with the Book

Mandela did not allow his spirit to be crushed by the harsh conditions in prison. He continued his struggle from within the prison walls despite many efforts by prison authorities and others to stop his resistance.

■ Something For The Time Being

> **READING CHECK**
>
> **a.** Daniel has lost his job because he is frequently imprisoned for months at a time.
>
> **b.** Flora Donaldson is a white woman who supports the fight against apartheid. She is the person who puts Daniel in contact with William Chadders.
>
> **c.** William cannot allow Daniel to wear his Congress button because it would cause problems with his business partner.

1. Ella and Daniel do not communicate with one another and have little common ground in their relationship. Daniel's frequent prison stays have caused tension and distance between them. Although Madge and William do communicate openly, they have similar tensions caused by their differing political views.

2. Responses will vary. Students may find William somewhat hypocritical or perhaps too easily intimidated. On the other hand, students should recognize that William may know best what strategy to employ in order to achieve large-scale, behind-the-scenes results.

3. Madge has realized that although both she and William believe that the apartheid laws are wrong and should be changed, they have very different ideas about how to change them. Madge suggests that these differences cause her to see part of William that she was previously unaware of.

Connecting with the Book

Like Mandela, Daniel is very aware of the political environment around him. Both men feel the need to be involved in the struggle for change. Daniel, however, does not have the benefit of an education and is therefore somewhat limited in his ability to contribute. Both men also suffer strain in their personal relationships as a result of their activism.

■ Oh, God, How Long Can We Go On? *and* Biko

> **READING CHECK**
>
> **a.** Steven Biko was killed for his activism in the struggle against apartheid.
>
> **b.** The UN imposed an arms embargo on South Africa as a result of Biko's death.
>
> **c.** Tutu says that people should be treated equally because "we are human persons" created in God's image.

1. Responses will vary. Students might suggest that the minister of police had no remorse about the death of Steve Biko.

2. Biko's death was so senseless and violent that it was indicative of the general conditions in South Africa. The murder of a promising and intelligent young man gained international attention because it was completely unjustified and because it was far from uncommon.

3. The lines from the song suggest that although the South African state was able to kill Steve Biko, it would not be able to stop the controversy and protest that his death had caused.

Connecting with the Book

Both events received worldwide protest. Biko's funeral was attended by representatives from several governments and was the cause of many protests, and the Rivonia trial caused the South African state to receive pressure from countries all over the world.

■ Sunlight in Trebizond Street

> **READING CHECK**
>
> **a.** The speaker has been in prison for over a hundred days.
>
> **b.** Casper wants the speaker to reveal his organization's leader.
>
> **c.** The speaker has formed a relationship with a woman outside the People's League.

1. The People's League is a political organization that is opposed to the government.

2. At the beginning of the story, the speaker is defiant and determined to resist Casper's questioning. By the end of the story, he is uncertain of his loyalty and has lost much of his courage.

3. Responses will vary. Students might suggest that the speaker will be killed by the People's League, or that he will be imprisoned again.

Connecting with the Book

While the speaker is dedicated to his resistance, his dedication falters. Mandela does not waver in his determination and suffers much more than the speaker in the story. The speaker is imprisoned for only a few months, whereas Mandela remains in prison for almost three decades. Also, Mandela continues his fight from prison, but the speaker thinks of little beyond his own personal suffering.

■ Saint Crispian Day Speech

> **READING CHECK**
> a. A battle is taking place during the speech.
> b. The men who do not fight will be ashamed that they missed the battle and will wish that they had participated.

1. The speech is meant to rally men for battle and to give them courage.

2. The speaker feels that the battle is necessary and is proud to be involved in it.

Connecting with the Book

Both speakers suggest that they are willing to die for the cause they are fighting for. They suggest that no matter how difficult and painful, the fight must continue, at all costs.

■ Prologue

> **READING CHECK**
> a. The speaker lives in Russia.
> b. The speaker goes insane.

1. The objects personified in the poem include moonlight, night, death, and madness.

2. The speaker's son is in prison and her husband has died.

3. Responses will vary. The students should suggest that the speaker and her son have a very close relationship and support the response with details from the poem.

Connecting with the Book

The speaker in the poem is completely desperate when her son is taken away from her. She begs for his release and is ultimately driven mad. Winnie continues to support Nelson, but she refrains from any show of emotion or weakness. The differences can be attributed to the fact that the speaker has no one but her son, whereas Winnie has children and friends to offer her support. Also, Nelson was not sentenced to death, whereas the speaker's son was.

■ South African Panel's Report . . .

> **READING CHECK**
> a. No political party supported the findings.
> b. The South African government committed the greatest number of human rights violations.
> c. The ANC is accused of attacking civilians, killing informers, and encouraging others to commit human rights violations.

1. Responses will vary. Those who submitted a complete confession were given amnesty.

2. The Truth and Reconciliation Committee's report was not accepted by any group as completely true and caused controversy, not reconciliation.

3. Responses will vary. Students may note that the political goals of the Inkatha are significantly different from the nonracial, democratic vision of the ANC.

Connecting with the Book

Responses will vary. Students may suggest that Mandela repeatedly says that the ANC resorted to violent tactics only when all other avenues of protest had failed. The accusations do not include any actions that the ANC would be opposed to, although Mandela says the organization was committed to trying to avoid harming innocent civilians. Other students may suggest that, although the ANC did sometimes use violence to achieve its goals, it had no other alternative; therefore, these actions should not be considered human rights violations, since the ANC was in fact fighting for human rights.

■ The Last White Man

READING CHECK
a. Most newly-independent African countries experienced economic ruin and political corruption.
b. Eighteen of the twenty poorest countries are in Africa.
c. The Afrikaners set up a deliberately inferior education system.

1. In the face of the facts he sets forth, the writer, though attempting to be somewhat objective, is not hopeful for Africa's future.
2. The statement suggests that the religions displaced by the "new god" were inferior.
3. The writer is implying that the black Africans are underproductive.

Connecting with the Book

Responses will vary. Students may note that Mandela, while painfully aware of the obstacles new governments face, would never give up hope.

■ Epilogue: Confronting the Ghosts

READING CHECK
a. Hendrik Verwoerd was the South African prime minister who played a key role in creating and maintaining white supremacy in South Africa.
b. Hendrik Verwoerd is the grandfather of Wilhelm Verwoerd.

1. White South Africans were forced to choose between the racist far right or the ANC. There was no longer middle ground because the issues had become so volatile that a compromise was nearly impossible.
2. Wilhelm's education removed him from the political environment of South Africa and forced him to look with an outsider's perspective. Also, his studies in philosophy probably had a great influence on the way he viewed apartheid.
3. If the past is forgotten, the lessons will also be forgotten. Also, there was a great amount of pain inflicted by apartheid that needed to be recognized in order for a reconciliation to be complete between the groups in South Africa.

Connecting with the Book

Mandela and others who fought for freedom in South Africa did not seek to gain freedom merely for themselves, but for all the people of South Africa. For the grandson of the man who championed apartheid to belong to the organization that led to apartheid's ultimate demise is the fulfillment of Mandela's mission. All people of South Africa were subjugated under the unjust laws, and all have benefited from their destruction.

Test

■ Part I: Objective Questions *(2 points each)*

1. F	6. T	11. d
2. F	7. F	12. b
3. F	8. F	13. c
4. T	9. T	14. a
5. F	10. T	15. d

Answer Key *(cont.)*

Long Walk to Freedom

■ Part II: Short-Answer Questions

(4 points each)

16. Mandela is dumbstruck by the poet's words. He is shocked that the poet considers the white man an "interloper" and is stirred by the poet's zealous nationalism.

17. When Mandela goes underground, he develops a reputation for being able to elude the police, and thus becomes known as "the Black Pimpernel"—an allusion to the fictional Scarlet Pimpernel, known for evading capture during the French Revolution.

18. Mandela, a pragmatist, believes a method should be used only as long as it is effective. When peaceful protest ceases to work, Mandela feels the ANC must take up arms and protect its people from the violent arm of the government.

19. Mandela tours the continent to solicit support for the ANC from other African leaders and to receive military training in Ethiopia.

20. While Mandela is driving back to Johannesburg after meeting with Chief Luthuli to report on his continental tour, police pull his car over and he is arrested and charged with illegal exit from the country.

21. He represents himself because he wants to take advantage of his symbolic status, and because he wants not to defend himself but to put the state on trial.

22. The most important person in any prisoner's life, according to Mandela, is the warder, because the warder has almost complete control over one's day-to-day existence.

23. Mandela lives in relative luxury—he has a private house and grounds, a live-in cook, and an open schedule. Yet he is still acutely aware that he remains a prisoner in an unjust society.

24. Mandela doesn't completely trust de Klerk and he often feels that de Klerk is intentionally stalling the negotiations, but he also realizes that to create change one must sometimes make a partner out of one's enemy.

25. The ANC wins the election and Nelson Mandela becomes president.

■ Part III: Essay Questions *(15 points each)*

a. Students may agree that great character is necessarily born out of great hardship, or they may argue that people who have lived relatively comfortable lives can also develop great character. Students may suggest that hardship is merely the context in which character is revealed. Responses should be supported by evidence taken from the book and also from history.

b. Responses will vary. Sacrifices Mandela makes include his bachelor's degree at Fort Hare; his law practice; his freedom (while in prison); both his marriages; his relationships with his mother, children, and grandchildren; and his private life (after his release). Students may suggest that one man's private life is a worthy price to pay for the liberation of millions of other lives.

c. Responses will vary. Students may consider such character traits as Mandela's commitment, his humility, his diplomacy, his dignity, his pragmatism, his idealism, his empathy, or his love of humanity. Responses should be supported with specific examples from the autobiography.

d. Responses will vary, but students will likely consider some or all of these clothing items: Mandela's first-day-of-school outfit—his father's trousers cut off at the knee; his first double-breasted suit; the leopard-skin kaross Mandela wears into court; and the short trousers worn by African prisoners. In each case, students should point out how the clothing item symbolizes identity, oppression, or the resistance of oppression.

e. Responses will vary according to class interaction with the **Connections** selections.

Notes

ISBN 0-03-056582-0 NB2I

90000

9 780030 565823

HOLT, RINEHART AND WINSTON